ROGER STAUBACH

Captain America

ROGER STAUBACH

Captain America

MIKE TOWLE

CUMBERLAND HOUSE
NASHVILLE, TENNESSEE

Published by
    Cumberland House Publishing, Inc.
    431 Harding Industrial Drive
    Nashville, TN 37211
    www.cumberlandhouse.com

Cover design by Gore Studio, Inc.

Library of Congress Cataloging-in-Publication Data

Roger Staubach : Captain America / [compiled by] Mike Towle.
    p. cm.
    ISBN 1-58182-305-3 (pbk. : alk. paper) ISBN 978-1-68442-250-0 (hc)
    1. Staubach, Roger, 1942—Anecdotes. 2. Staubach, Roger, 1942—Friends
and associates. 3. Football players—United States—Biography. I. Towle,
Mike.
    GV939.S733 A3 2002
    796.332'092—dc21

                                                        2002010382

CONTENTS

To Uncle Bill and Aunt Susie

ACKNOWLEDGMENTS

Thanks to the following for allowing me to speak with them for this book: Tom Bates, Steve Belicheck, Joe Bellino, Gil Brandt, Bill Busik, Jack Clary, Larry Cole, Bo Coppedge, Pat Donnelly, Vince Eysoldt, Gene Ferrara, Rick Forzano, Walt Garrison, Bob Gramann, Dale Hansen, Wayne Hardin, Jim Heiselmann, Calvin Hill, Lee Roy Jordan, Bob Lilly, Frank Luksa, Tom Lynch, Mike McCoy, Don Meredith, Jerry Momper, Skip Orr, Drew Pearson, Myron Pottios, Dan Reeves, Pat Richter, Tex Schramm, Stan Sheppard, Roger Staubach, L. Budd Thalman, Jerry Tubbs, and Gaylord Ward.

As I was putting this book together, I spent some time on the telephone with Tom Bates, a former sports information director at Annapolis. Tom was extremely gracious and generous with his time in helping me track down some names and phone numbers of United States Naval Academy people who knew Roger, even though this was not a good time for Tom. He was dying of cancer, yet insisted on helping me out as best he could. He didn't know me from Adam, but that didn't matter. Tom passed away several weeks later. May God's eternal peace comfort his soul.

Gaylord Ward, one of Roger's classmates from Purcell High School, went the extra mile in allowing me to peruse all four of his high school yearbooks and his school's alumni directory. Classmates.com also proved helpful when it came to making initial contact with Staubach's Purcell classmates. I am also grateful to Roger Staubach himself for not only consenting to an interview in his Dallas office on a Monday afternoon for this unauthorized book but also for his help in putting me in touch with many of the people interviewed for this book. Thank you, Sharon Bell, for putting me through to Roger.

The media relations folks at the Dallas Cowboys and the Naval Academy opened their doors and their files to me, and were generous in allowing me to use photos that appear in this book. At the Cowboys, I thank Rich Dalrymple, Brett Daniels, and Scott Agulnek. At the Naval Academy, my thanks go to Scott Strasemeier.

Thanks to everyone at Cumberland House, especially publisher Ron Pitkin and editor John Mitchell, for making this a worthy venture.

None of this would be possible without my wife, Holley, and son, Andrew, two of God's many gifts to me.

As always, thank You, Jesus Christ, for Your saving grace.

INTRODUCTION

*I*T MUST BE NIFTY being Roger Staubach. He retired from America's team as "Captain America," and here he is nearly a quarter-century later still being used by staunch Cowboys fanatics as the measuring stick for all Cowboys quarterbacks recent past, present, and future. He owns a Heisman Trophy; is married to his lovely hometown sweetheart, with whom he has raised five great kids; is devoted to God and bold about his Christian faith; and can get great seats whenever he goes to a game.

Staubach also has carved out a terrific second career as the founding owner of a multimillion-dollar company that bears his name and now employs a number of his good friends from the three C's: hometown Cincy, college, and the Cowboys. It's nice to have friends, isn't it—ones who knew you and laughed or cried with you *before* you became rich and famous? Friends who served Mass with you while you were in grade school? Friends who were there to hold you up during a relentlessly plebeian year of harassment and regimentation at Annapolis? Friends who encouraged you after you separated a shoulder in the 1972 preseason when it looked like you were *finally* going to be the Cowboys' starter?

Staubach is a grandpa now, and he wears his age well. At age sixty he remains ruggedly handsome, engaging, and lean and unmean. He still has the right touch in being able to disarm strangers without trying, and he can still throw a football hard and accurately enough to make you think he could still be playing pro football even today. Just maybe—if he were limited to a couple dozen snaps a game and with a few more rules concessions in place about protecting quarterbacks.

Rap sheet? Are you kidding? This is an altar boy, still, sans cassock. Song sheet, perhaps, but not a rap sheet.

What's there not to like about being Roger Staubach? Nothing, unless you count the things you *can't* do in public. Such as getting through a complete meal at the restaurant without signing a few napkins. Or opening his mouth to speak about his faith, or raising a hand in prayer, and being labeled a "religious fanatic" by some poor soul across the room. Or downing a brew or a glass of wine after another scrappy game of three-on-three hoops and wondering if someone watching will get the wrong idea.

Three things that you will never see Roger Staubach do in public: lay rubber, throw a golf club, pick his nose.

When Staubach retired from the Cowboys after the 1979 season, he left the game as its highest-rated passer of all time, a six-time Pro Bowler who had led Dallas to two Super Bowl titles and was around for three other Super Bowl games. This from a guy who was better known at Navy as a scrambler than a passer, who didn't play pro football until after he had been out of college four years, and whose best aptitude for sports may actually have resided in baseball.

He was just thirty-seven when he played his last game, a 1979 playoff loss to the Los Angeles Rams. It was a young thirty-seven if you don't count all the concussions. Those four interim years in the navy made him an old rookie when he got to the Cowboys in 1969, but that football sabbatical also meant those were four years his body wasn't being beat up by the likes of Dick Butkus, Alan Page, and Jack Lambert.

Even with the late start, things kept getting later and later for Staubach. For the first half of Staubach's eleven seasons with the Cowboys, head coach Tom Landry often waffled between quarterbacks, going back and forth between Roger the Dodger and Craig Morton. Respective injuries often played a part in determining not so much who *would* or *should* play as to who *could* play, but indecision on the part of Landry factored into the equation for a long time.

For goodness' sake, in 1971 Staubach and Morton even alternated plays in one game. Actually, it wasn't so good: The Chicago Bears beat the Cowboys, 23-19. On the other hand, Staubach then took over and led the Cowboys to ten straight victories, culminating in a Super Bowl triumph over the Miami Dolphins.

Even when Staubach became the starter for good—and that wasn't until 1973—there was the issue of his wanting to call his own plays. That wasn't going to happen with the cold, calculating Tom Landry and the ironclad Landry System. Landry and Staubach shared some of the same basic tenets when it came to their Christian beliefs (Landry was a Methodist, Staubach a Catholic), but personal salvation is one thing, giving Staubach every-down license to do things his way was another. Staubach wanted the keys to the car, but Dad wouldn't give 'em up.

More than two decades have passed since Staubach retired from football, giving plenty of time for knowledge of his upbringing and football career to baste in the minds of those who have known him best. *Roger Staubach, Captain America*, is not the authoritative biography of the Pro Football Hall of Famer; rather, it is more a literary scrapbook, a collection of hundreds of memories, stories, insights, and analyses of Roger Staubach from many sides and angles.

All together, these firsthand accounts of life with Staubach bear out that while it might, in fact, be nifty to be Roger Staubach, it came with the price of hard work, an unwavering faith, loyal comrades, and a few good breaks along the way.

ROGER STAUBACH

Captain America

THE CINCINNATI KID

*R*OGER STAUBACH WAS BORN on February 5, 1942, as an only child to Robert and Elizabeth Staubach, and he grew up in the Cincinnati suburb of Silverton. There was nothing extraordinary about his coming into the world, his rearing, his childhood achievements, his Catholic faith, or his choice of extracurricular activities. He was a good student, not a brilliant one; a good athlete, not a superstar; and he was a good friend to many, not a stuck-up elitist.

Bob and Betty provided young Roger with a loving home, a middle-class upbringing blanketed in warmth and security, and the freedom and encouragement to chase the American Dream. Theirs was a disciplined household as well as a nurturing one, a safe haven where Roger Staubach could enjoy life, liberty, and the pursuit of happiness. It was there that he inherited and added to a foundation of faith in God and Jesus Christ as well as a Midwestern work ethic that equipped him well for a success-oriented world in a day and age where shades of gray didn't cut it.

PURCELL HIGH SCHOOL CAVALIER

A young Captain America.

It was in Cincinnati and at Purcell High School, an inner-city parochial Catholic school with insufficient acreage for its own sports fields, that Staubach planted his roots. They still run deep. He grew up in the fifties and came of age in that period of time between the end of the Korean War and the beginning of the Kennedy presidency. Elvis Presley was king, Joseph McCarthy was on a tear, *Sputnik* was in space, the A-bomb was standing by, and the James Dean influence was in full bloom with leather jackets and ducktails. It was a time for hot cars and the Cold War.

Then there was this straight-arrow Staubach kid who was soon making a name for himself around Ohio as a three-sport star. If he hadn't gone on to play pro football, he might have been a long shot to make it in the NBA and an odds-on favorite to make it all the way to Major League Baseball, perhaps either with the hometown Reds or those Indians up north. The altar boy was becoming an altered young man, square by today's outlandish standards but well-grounded, well-groomed, and well-liked among his Purcell peers.

Roger met his bride-to-be, Marianne Hoobler, while they were both in grade school, around the same time he was getting his first taste of athletic lofty achievement as part of a Knothole baseball team that won a national championship.

One of many Staubach traits that emerged in Cincinnati—and one that has stayed with him his whole life—is his continued friendship with a number of his hometown acquaintances. He has long since moved on and out of Ohio, but he has done well to stay in touch with friends, and they with him. At least once every year or two, Roger and Marianne make it a point to get together with his high school buddies, such as Vince Eysoldt, Jerry Momper, and Stan Sheppard, and their wives. It's pretty much the same with Staubach's Naval Academy brethren, such as Tom Lynch, Edward "Skip" Orr, and Pat Donnelly, among others. Ditto for former Dallas Cowboys teammates. When it's time to get together, it's often Roger and Marianne who play host at their summer home near Austin, Texas.

Few bridges have been burned in this unpretentious guy's life.

BETTY STAUBACH, *Roger's mom:*

We were given only one child, but God gave us a good one.[1]

VINCE EYSOLDT *met Staubach in 1948, when they were first-graders at Saint John's Catholic Grade School. It is a friendship that has stood the test of time:*

We were both athletic and liked doing the same kind of things. We did almost everything together: baseball, basketball, and football. We were both altar boys. We were on a relay bicycle-racing team. In baseball, I was the pitcher and he was the catcher when we won the national championship in Class B Knothole.

Roger's dad was a Little League coach. Roger had great fond memories of his parents, who were disciplinarians. He had to take piano lessons when none of the rest of us did.

We did all the common things together, and we weren't always saints. Back then, a big thing was knocking on someone's front door and running, and going around shooting peashooters.

We did all the rowdy, little-boy things, but nothing severe or really bad.

Roger always did the right thing. He would stick up for what he believed in, and that was one of the things I really admired him for. If somebody took a position on an issue that he disagreed with, he stood up for his point of view. He remained true to his convictions. That goes back to his having a close relationship with his parents and having respect for authority in general. He never questioned it when a coach told him to take a lap or whatever. He would accept a punishment whether he deserved it or not.

To be a friend to Staubach, as EYSOLDT *discovered, sometimes meant having to put on the thick skin, or at least not to be so gullible:*

Roger and I were altar boys together. I remember one morning having to go to my first assignment of serving a Mass. He was the lead altar boy at our parish, so he was there with me.

I hadn't studied properly for the Mass. You had to know Latin to understand what the priest was doing and when it was the proper time to ring the bells. The bells were supposed to be rung at a very holy or solemn time, and I certainly didn't want to be ringing them at the wrong time. Ringing the bells usually meant it was time to stand up if you were kneeling or sitting down, or vice versa.

So I asked Roger that morning to help me out because I was a little confused. And this was the early morning Mass, when most of the nuns and other priests were there to get their daily Mass obligation out of the way early so they could get to work. Everyone would be watching.

Roger said, "Don't worry about it. Just keep looking at me, and I'll nod my head when it's time for you to ring the bells."

So during the Mass, I would look over and see Roger nodding his head. I would ring the bells and hear the accompanying commotion behind me as the people stood up or sat down together. Of course, I ended up ringing the bell an all-time high. You were supposed to ring the bells a total of about three times during the Mass, and I think I must have rung them fifteen. I had people sitting, standing, sitting again, and moving around . . . they must have thought that the rules for the Mass had been changed. I got into a lot of trouble after it was all over.

EYSOLDT *remembers how their athletic exploits sometimes ran into obstacles along the way:*

Our eighth-grade baseball team was going to the city championship—we had beaten every team in our league by a landslide. Our coach said meet at four at the school because we have a five-thirty game. We got a call that told us, "Don't come down, because your game was at two." So we had to forfeit the city-championship game through no fault of our own. Our coach was kind of a goofy guy.

No one came close to beating us in football our eighth-grade year. But because one of our players didn't weigh in, we had to forfeit the entire season. I didn't play that season because we had a weight limit of 125 pounds, and I weighed more than that. Then, in high school, we played all sports together and there were no things like weight limits.

BETTY STAUBACH:

Rog would be the last person to think of himself as a leader, and he's been like this as long as I can remember. When Rog first started playing for the Saint John's Boys Club in grade school, his coach, Paul Riesenberg, told me, "Boy, Rog should be a quarterback. He has the mind and the know-how to lead that team. But Rog doesn't *want* to be a quarterback. He wants to be an end or a halfback. He wants to run with the ball. So I guess I won't make him a quarterback."[2]

Like Eysoldt, JERRY MOMPER is one of Roger's old-time friends from Purcell. Although they didn't meet until they were teenagers "trying out" for football together, Momper relates that it was more "trying" for him than it was for the athletic whiz kid:

My first memory of him was freshman year in high school and getting into line on the football field with about 125 kids trying out for the freshman football team. This was my first introduction to Roger because I hadn't known him in grade school. He originally was a wide receiver and also played defensive back. Toward the end of the sophomore year, he broke a wrist and was also moved to quarterback.

I had an older brother who went to Purcell, and he said to me, "Jer, this is what I recommend you do: Go out for center because no one likes to play center." I played linebacker on defense. Because I was the center, Roger and I worked together quite a bit, especially on his conversion from playing defense to playing quarterback. Coach McCarthy had very strict rules on just how he wanted the snap count to work, so we would work for hours just on that aspect.

The one thing that always impressed me when Roger was quarterback was his command of the huddle. There was no question who was the boss in the huddle, even though you always had guys wanting to put their own two cents in. He was the kind of guy you just wanted to do well for.

Because Purcell was an inner-city school, it didn't have room enough on its own property for athletic fields.

STAN SHEPPARD, *another high school pal, remembers the daily off-campus excursions just so the football team could have a place to practice:*

As freshmen, we practiced in a place called the Owl's Nest, an old, dried-up lakebed. It could get really, early hot, and we could see the wind blow over the top and we wouldn't get any of it. And there was no grass; it was all dirt. It was tough, man, I'll tell you what. Whoever came out of there was tough.

We would have to walk at least two miles to get to Owl's Nest.

Staubach as a sophomore, working the shot that can still be often seen in his driveway at home in Dallas.

We'd get our gym shoes on, carry our football cleats, and walk to the Owl's Nest every day during the week, and then put on our cleats there. When we walked back, I can remember being so thirsty that we'd stop at everybody's yard that had a faucet, and we knew exactly where every faucet was. Staubach was right there getting water along with everybody else. When you think about it, this was the kind of stuff that made us a great team. That was true camaraderie.

SHEPPARD *recalls how he and Staubach, as sophomores, got hurt—on the same day, no less:*

Roger broke a hand in a hard practice we were put through after we lost a game, and losing wasn't much fun at Purcell. I got a hand stepped on in the same practice, and that's when we were using the old metal cleats. They had to put clamps and stitches in mine, so I missed a couple of weeks, too.

By the time they were juniors, they had graduated from the Owl's Nest to the varsity, and that meant a bus ride every day. SHEPPARD:

During our junior and senior years, we had to get on a bus and travel thirty-five to forty minutes to get to a place called Lunken Airport. That's where the varsity practiced. It's an airport in Cincinnati that is huge. They took the varsity down there in two buses, and then they'd go back to get the sophomores.

When they told you to run, you ran until you were out of sight. And we didn't have water. We practiced for two and a half or three hours. I never got home during football season until seven-thirty or eight at night. That wasn't the worst of it: Roger lived in the Silverton area, which was another ten to fifteen miles beyond where I lived.

One night our junior year, we got beat on a rainy night that was so bad, halfway through the game we had to change our quarterback and center, so that Roger and Jerry Momper switched over from defense. This was done because Roger had the biggest hands and could hold onto the football. It rained so hard that we had standing water on a field that was crowned.

Not all of the high school fun was confined to the football field, as SHEPPARD *recalls:*

As a junior, Roger was one of the few guys who had a car—his parents had gotten it for him—and it was a four-door. He was driving a bunch of us home, and we all piled into the car. One of the other guys, Mike Wirth, who played linebacker, with some help from Vince Eysoldt, had put a smoke bomb under the hood of the car.

When Roger turned the key, the bomb went off and it made a really loud noise. Smoke was pouring out of everywhere, and Staubach jumped out of the car. He went to the back of the car, having no idea what was wrong. The only thing he knew about cars was how to get gas and where to put it in. He had no mechanical skills. Give him a screwdriver or a hand-held drill, and he's liable to hurt himself.

He looked under the back of the car, where most of the smoke was coming out, and he thought it was the transmission. Mike and Vince were on the ground, they were laughing so hard.

EYSOLDT:

We were a bit more naïve in those days. Roger goes, "Oh, no, I forgot to put oil into it, and now my parents are going to kill me." He went on and on, not knowing any better.

What happened with those smoke bombs is that they had a fuse that could be rigged to be attached to a spark plug, and when you turned the key to start the car it would set the bomb off. And we didn't have locking hoods in those days, so it was easy for someone to get in there and plant a smoke bomb or whatever— but not something really dangerous. Unless you were a car jockey, all you knew about cars was where the gas tank was and how to put gas into it.

Although Staubach's best buddies in Cincinnati were jock-oriented, he was popular with most of his fellow students. They got to see plenty of him, especially when the whole student body ate lunch together in the school cafeteria, allowing all the different

*classes to intermingle. It was always a hot meal. Classmate
GAYLORD WARD recalls Staubach as the kind of guy who could
show empathy for someone even while he was ribbing them:*

My stepfather is the man I considered my real dad, and his name
was William Means. My mother remarried when I was six years
old, but, of course, I kept Ward for my last name. As I got to know
Roger, he had somewhere seen that my parents' last name was
Means, and he picked up on this discrepancy in names and asked
me, "Means? Who the heck is Means?"

I said, "He's my dad."

And Roger asked, "Then why do you have a different last
name?"

"Well, I'm being raised by my stepfather and that's his name.
Ward is the name of my birth father."

We had this exchange a number of times, and each time at the
end Roger would just kind of shake his head. There was a little
family history there. Yeah, he was razzing me in some respects and
probably a little perplexed at the same time. Whatever it was, it was
done in good nature. There was nothing cruel about how he did it.

There weren't many kids in that school who came from what you
might call broken families or with a parent who had remarried.
Divorce was fairly uncommon back then, especially among Catholics.

*By the time he was a senior, WARD was big enough to play
sports—if only he'd had the time:*

By the end of my senior year I was six-foot-one and weighed 185
pounds. I can remember Coach McCarthy coming to me and
saying, "Hey, we need people like you on the football team." I was
larger than a lot of players on the football team, but I told Coach,
"I can't play because I have to work (after school) to earn money."
He said, "You're going to have your whole life after you get out of
school to work." I said, "You don't understand. My stepfather is

doing a great job raising me and providing for us, but I pay for the school tuition and all of my books."

I worked from the fourth grade on all the way through high school delivering papers. By the time I was in high school doing this, I had three younger guys working for me. I would drive the truck and spot the papers for them around town. I did this all the way through my first year at the University of Cincinnati. I started out making about two bucks a week, and by the time I was eighteen I was making about twenty-five a week.

There were two parts to this. One was that my stepfather wanted to instill in me a strong work ethic. Another was the money situation. My parents didn't have a whole lot of money, certainly not enough to be able to send me to a private school. Very few of the students at Purcell had their dads working in a civil service job, like my stepdad did. Most of the other fathers were businessmen or lawyers or things like that.

It didn't bother me at all. There were benefits to working. When I was sixteen years old, I bought a car and was able to drive to school. When Roger saw the car, he asked me whose car it was. I told him that I bought it, and he exclaimed, "How were you able to buy it? Where did you get the money?" I said, "I earned it!"

I remember that car well. It was a '38 Buick Roadmaster that I paid fifty bucks for. The transmission went out about two months after I bought it, and it was going to cost me three hundred dollars to fix it. My dad told me to get a motor manual and buy some tools, and that's what I did. I fixed it myself, but it still wasn't right. So I took it apart again and did it right the second time. Worked like a charm.

GENE FERRARA *was another of Staubach's classmates:*

We had twelve hundred students there, and they were all boys. We had some pretty good sports teams because there were so many boys to choose from.

All I had ever wanted to do was play football. But as a freshman, I was five-foot-seven and weighed about 125 pounds. On the first day of practice, all the prospective players went out into the schoolyard and lined up alphabetically. I'm standing next to Vince Eysoldt. I'm looking over at him, and there's Vince, about six-foot-one and weighing around 190 pounds. The coaches kind of glanced right over me and went straight to Vince, as if to say to me, "Sorry, but you're just not a football player."

By the time I was a sophomore, I started getting involved in track and then some other activities, and that's how I came to know Roger. What I remember most about the high school is the number of activities that they had. I guess the priests were trying to keep us busy so we wouldn't think about girls. There were a ton of things to get involved in. Even if you didn't want to get into sports, they had things like the American History Club, drama, student council, the school newspaper, and Sodality, which was a religious organization. I found out that you found most of the same people in all of these different activities.

You had to wear a tie at the school. There were some godawful combinations of shirts and ties. You couldn't wear jeans. We had a vice principal by the name of Brother Larry Everslade, who was about six-four and 230, who was in charge of discipline, so discipline was pretty tight. We also had a demerit system—if you got a certain number, you got detention and had to stay after school. The school had a code and you were expected to abide by it.

Roger was pretty strait-laced. I never saw him get into any kind of trouble, and I say that not because they gave him favor but because he just wasn't that kind of person. He wasn't rowdy and never called attention to himself except in a positive way.

Athletics was a year-round proposition for the serious jocks.
STAN SHEPPARD:

In the summertime, once we got to be juniors, we always hung out at a place called the DAV—the Disabled American Veterans. They had this really big softball field with a big hill, and that's where we would work out, throwing the ball and running to get in shape. We'd all meet down there periodically throughout the week, and it was all done on our own. We had fifteen to twenty guys working out all the time.

VINCE EYSOLDT *loved competing with—and against— Staubach, and vice versa:*

PURCELL HIGH SCHOOL CAVALIER

Staubach's scrambling exploits were already legend in his high school years.

Roger and I were best of friends through high school, although we were competitive with one another. Who would score the most points in basketball? Who would get the most hits in baseball?

Coach Jim McCarthy was very much a disciplinarian, someone you would not talk to. If you saw him coming down the hall, you would try not to look up because he wouldn't talk to you anyway. Back in those days, the coach was the supreme power, and you did what he said.

I remember that for one game against one of our rivals, unbeknownst to anybody else, Roger worked it out somehow with the backfield coach that he would do a naked reverse around the opposite side of where the line and the backs were going. It was called a 28 Power Sweep to the Right. I would normally carry the ball on that play. As we broke the huddle and walked to the line, Roger turned to me and said, "Act like you have the ball because I'm going to fake it to you."

I went up to the line of scrimmage thinking, *Oh, boy, this guy has just signed his death warrant. Finally, I can get even with him for the ringing of the bells. He's going to hang in the schoolyard.* The ball was snapped, and Roger faked putting the ball into my stomach, although I acted like I still had it and took off around right end. When I got across the line, I got absolutely smeared, cleated, and killed. But I heard this loud cheer. Roger had kept it and taken it all the way around the left side, and he ran seventy yards, untouched, for the touchdown.

That was so unlike our football team because we were so much a three-yards-and-a-cloud-of-dust team. We were powerful and bigger than anyone else, so we were able to push the ball down the field. Maybe Coach McCarthy knew about the play, but when it was all said and done, I'm sure he was happy about it, and I'm pretty sure that Roger didn't get disciplined for it.

Anyway, we won the game, and that's the way Roger was. In basketball he would always want to take the last shot. He thrived under those kinds of conditions. He may not always win or be the strongest and the toughest, but he would always fight to the very end and want to do more after that.

He was the prom king, and I was the first or second runner-up. He was class president, and I was vice president. We grew up in those kinds of roles.

STAN SHEPPARD:

I'll tell you how upset Coach McCarthy was; he put that play in for our next ball game.

JERRY MOMPER:

Roger and I were co-captains our senior year, which was a tough year for me because I broke my collarbone twice that year, the first time playing tag football and then again on the last play of a scrimmage. It was tough sitting on the bench as a co-captain, but fortunately it didn't stop me from getting a college football scholarship.

Our last game that year was against Roger Bacon, another Catholic school in the city. They had a coach who was ahead of our coach. Our coach, Jim McCarthy, had the reputation and the talent, but Bacon's coach knew a few more innovative things. We wound up losing, 9-6, with Roger running for what we thought would be the winning score, only to get tackled on the two-yard line as time ran out.

That was in a stadium that held about four thousand people, and there were about ten or eleven thousand people there watching the game, sitting on the surrounding hills.

ROGER STAUBACH *pipes in:*

Purcell had a great football program, and we were competitive every year. Our coach, Jim McCarthy, switched me to quarterback my senior year. The way it was set up there was that the juniors played defense and the seniors played offense, and very few sophomores played. I broke my hand sophomore year and then played defense my junior year, so my senior year really was my first year of being the Purcell quarterback.

We ran from the T formation and didn't really throw the ball all that much. Even on some of our passing plays I ended up running quite a bit. So by the end of my senior year no one really knew if I was a good passer or if I was a runner. They knew I was a good quarterback athletically, but they couldn't really figure me out.

PURCELL HIGH SCHOOL CAVALIER

Staubach, right, and Ohio State coach Woody Hayes met when Hayes visited Purcell as a guest speaker. Roger's classmate and buddy Jerry Momper is in the middle.

Ohio State coach Woody Hayes went after me, but I told him I wanted to throw more, and he said he would change things. I visited Purdue and ended up signing a letter of intent to go there. If I went to the Big Ten, it was going to be to Purdue. I had also visited Michigan and Indiana and had talked to Northwestern as well.

Notre Dame didn't really talk to me. A fullback who had played with me at Purcell and was older, Chuck Lima, had gone to Notre Dame, and he took film of me to show them and told them that they needed to talk to me. They told him that their quarterback quota was full and they didn't need another quarterback. I really would have been interested in Notre Dame, but that's as far as it went.

I then played in this North-South high school all-star football game, which also included Paul Warfield, among others. I played defensive back, wide receiver, and quarterback in that game. It was played in June, and after the game Notre Dame called and offered me a scholarship. But I had committed to going to the Naval Academy after I completed a year at this junior college, New Mexico Military Institute. What this all boiled down to was, I was actually spending a redshirt year at New Mexico. It gave me another year to think about things, even though I went off with the idea that I was going to be going to the Naval Academy.

I really improved a lot that year, and part of that is that I was able to throw a lot at New Mexico. We went 9-1 with a bunch of guys headed to the service academies, and we were ranked one of the top junior-college teams in the country. By then, colleges from all over the country were after me, but I stayed with the Naval Academy.

JIM HEISELMANN *wasn't a Purcell jock in the Staubach-Eysoldt-Momper mode, but he was a sports fan:*

One interesting angle about Roger's high school days was that both Roger and Pete Rose grew up in Cincinnati, were raised Catholic, and graduated around the same time, circa 1960. And, of course, both were outstanding athletes. Roger grew up on the east side of Cincy and Pete on the west. You can ask anyone from Cincinnati and they will tell you that there was a distinct difference in style between those two sides of town.

Roger stayed close to his roots and remained a hero over the years. Pete stayed close to his roots for years, even spending much of his major league career with the Cincinnati Reds—then strayed and now is considered by many to be a blight on the face of sports, a view I don't happen to share. I think Pete has some problems, but as a sports figure he was one of the greatest. A comparison of those two guys done in great detail would be very interesting.

Cincinnati in the late fifties offered plenty for teenagers to do on the weekend, and most of it had nothing to do with beer or cigarettes. GAYLORD WARD:

Saturday night was date night. We were fortunate because we had a place called Castle Farms, which featured big-name bands playing there. That was where you learned to dance, and it was fabulous. You could buy a ticket at the gate. One stipulation was that you had to be dressed in a tux, and all of us owned tuxes.

I lived in Mount Lookout. Roger lived up in the Pleasant Ridge area, which was more toward the northwest part of Cincinnati. There was a whole group of guys from the Ridge, and about the only time we mingled with each other was either at a school activity or at Castle Farms. That was where we spent most Saturday nights during the winter.

In the summertime, our favorite spot was Coney Island, which had Moonlight Gardens. That was an outdoor pavilion that also had the big bands. You could rent canoes and take your date out on Coney Island Lake, which was a shallow man-made lake, only about three feet deep, and they had lights all around the lake. This was right on the bank of the Ohio River. It was great.

Years later, while I was a firefighter in California, I would talk to the other guys about our days growing up, and some of these guys would tell me how much they hated their childhood. I couldn't believe it, because mine was *fabulous*. I guess it all depends on what we had available to us that determines what kind of memories we have about our youth.

VINCE EYSOLDT:

I remember being at a dance one time and there's Roger out there dancing in his own unique style. All I can say is that a bouncer came out and tried to grab Roger's tongue, thinking he was having some kind of seizure. He didn't have all the great moves and maneuvers like today's athletes do.

Actually, all of us were kind of spazzing out there on the dance floor, at least compared to today's kids. Jiminy Christmas. I guess Roger has picked up a little rhythm along the way, and I hear he learned how to dance a little bit—he can at least do the Texas Two-Step, although I don't know how well compared to real Texans.

GAYLORD WARD, *on growing up in the fifties:*

In those days the big worry was the A-bomb and what would happen with all the radiation if they dropped the bomb on us. The other thing that affected us was the Berlin Crisis, the Berlin Airlift. What that did to us in Hamilton County, Ohio, is that all of us who were going to graduate in 1960 and go on to college were supposed to have deferments from the draft. But the government removed the deferments, and so all of us were left scrambling to find a way to avoid the draft.

All the ROTC units were full. The Coast Guard didn't have a base around there. Then there was the Marine Corps, which had a PLC program for training leaders. So a bunch of us got into that. You would incur a three-year obligation after graduating from college. A bunch of us discussed this and agreed it was a better option than leaving ourselves open to the draft at that particular time.

VINCE EYSOLDT *remembers his high school years as a time when parents were truly involved in their children's school activities and how it didn't hurt to have a couple of usable thumbs:*

The program was, you thumbed [a ride] to school, you went to class, you had a break from all this drudgery at lunchtime, when you could play around and push and throw pretzels and all that. Then you got back to the serious work of class, and then afterward you went down to the locker room, changed clothes, went out onto the field, practiced, came back to the locker room, showered, put your clothes back on with your hair still wet, and your hair froze while you were out thumbing to get a ride home. Then you got home, studied, went to bed, and then it started all over again the next morning.

Parents would go to the games, and they would also go to film sessions on Wednesday night to see the plays and where the blocks were made and all that. It was kind of a social outing for the parents, so it was a community effort. A lot of parents could go to this because back then life on the job was nine to five, and then they were free to visit the school. Our parents were average, hard-working Americans. There were no blue bloods.

EYSOLDT *sums up Staubach and Purcell High:*

He had sparks of greatness as a high school football player, but he wasn't someone that you would say had All-American ability. After all, he only played quarterback his senior year, really. How well can you determine how great a guy is going to be at quarterback when he only started at that position ten times while in high school? But he did have some ability as well as deceptive speed. He was probably better as a basketball player, but limited by his height.

His goodness and belief system were between his ears. He was a good Christian guy. Back then, there wasn't much premarital sex in high school, not anything like now. That was especially true with athletes because you didn't have time for that.

It was a fairly strict school with a dress code. Every day it was slacks, a dress shirt, and a tie. Back then the teachers could correct you physically, and there were no lawsuits or this or that. If you got it, you deserved it.

It was a predominantly white, middle-class school. The average family income was around $6,000 to $10,000 a year, with most families being one-car families. Most of us had to thumb rides to get to school; it was ten or twelve miles from home. We didn't have a car, so we would have to stick our thumb out. Today you call it hitchhiking, but back then we called it thumbing. The interesting thing was, once you started school, you didn't see your house in the daylight again. You started out early in the morning when it was still dark and wouldn't get home until it was night. You had to hitch a ride to get down there, and after school you had practice for either football, basketball, or baseball.

There was no such thing as drugs, although we might read about it being a problem in another part of town. Things were a lot simpler then. I don't even know of any of the players smoking cigarettes in those days, and very

PURCELL HIGH SCHOOL CAVALIER

Roger, as king of the junior prom, with Marianne.

occasionally there might have been some beer somewhere. If the coaches found out about it—and you lived under a microscope back then—then the coaches would have you running laps until you couldn't run anymore; you'd be puking your guts out.

Roger and I lived about three blocks away from each other, and we would thumb to school together. We'd walk up to the corner, stick our thumbs out, and get a ride. It would be different people picking us up, but we saw a lot of the same faces. It would often be businessmen heading into town to go to their offices or some upperclassmen or teachers—it was a myriad of different people who would pick you up. It was a different way of life then—your thumb was your transportation, and you could get into a car then without fear of getting abducted, raped, shot, or otherwise attacked.

When we got older and our parents had another way of getting to work, then we could sometimes drive the family car. And there were three of us in the area who would take turns driving, depending on who had a car available to use. Everyone would chip in a quarter because you could buy a gallon of gas for a quarter back then—actually, five gallons for a dollar.

EYSOLDT, *on girls:*

Everyone had kind of a favorite, but interest in girls wasn't a driving force for us. Roger and Marianne (Hoobler) had been sort of an item, friends, since grade school. They were boyfriend and girlfriend, off and on, and they liked one another. But everyone sort of took for granted that once we got out of high school, everything would change and we'd all go our separate ways.

Roger and Marianne stayed together, although it wasn't always rosy. They broke up on different occasions. Their lives after high school were different: She was in nursing school, and he was away at the Naval Academy. They always stuck together and were perfect for each other.

Sports at Purcell wasn't just football. Most of Staubach's best friends played all three of the biggies—football, basketball, and baseball. JERRY MOMPER:

In those days, you played football in the fall, and as soon as that was over you started basketball practice. And as soon as basketball season was over, you either played baseball or ran track. A lot of people felt—and he may have felt this, too—that his best potential might have been in baseball because he batted over .400 at the Naval Academy. He had those long, lanky legs, which explains his nickname, "the Ostrich." He had a heckuva gait on him and was a terrific baseball player.

BOB GRAMANN, *another of Staubach's classmates, recalls one of the most incredible things he ever saw Staubach do in an athletic contest, and it didn't involve football:*

Staubach goes hard into third playing baseball his sophomore year.

One of the most amazing things I saw him do occurred on the baseball diamond, not on a football field. It was the time that Roger got caught in a rundown between second and third base. These guys had him dead, with the play well backed up and no mishandling of the ball. Yet, all of a sudden, there's Roger safe at third after diving back into the bag. I swear he was heading back toward second at one point, when all of a sudden he had reversed direction and gone into third, untagged. Unbelievable. I've never again seen such a move on the base paths at any level of the game. You knew right then there was something pretty special about this guy.

STAN SHEPPARD:

During baseball season, we used to throw in the gym to get loosened up, and the coaches would stand behind us because we were a little wild. We would both throw the ball hard, and it would go flying over our heads and be rattling around in the gym, hurting some of the coaches.

Time out for a checkup on Staubach's academic progress.
VINCE EYSOLDT:

He wasn't a genius or in advanced classes, but he was a good student. If there was homework or studying to do, he would do it. He wouldn't overstudy or overdo it, but he would pay attention in the classroom. If you didn't, the outcome wasn't good because the teachers really had authority in those days. There was no such thing as skipping class.

GENE FERRARA:

What I remember most about him is that even with all the city-wide attention he got, none of that affected how he treated other people. I was always comfortable talking with him—I never got the sense that he thought of himself as anything special. As an example of that, after he graduated from the Naval Academy, he remained in Annapolis on assignment for a while before going to Vietnam. My wife and I were on vacation in Washington, D.C., around that time, and I got his phone number and called him. I wanted to see if there was any chance that we could come out and have him get us onto the base so we could see it. He said sure, and he made all the arrangements for us.

We drove out there and met him. He spent several hours with us that afternoon taking us all around the base, showing us everything. Basically, he interrupted his day on no notice to accommodate us. Here he is, a Heisman Trophy winner and Naval Academy graduate, and I'm just some guy who went to high school with him, and he's treating me like I was his best friend.

That really impressed me, but it was typical Roger. I've always told people that.

A few years later he was at our tenth high school reunion, and a paperback book on him had just come out. He graciously autographed a copy of the book, and even then he never acted like he was anything special. And that's what made him special.

A look back at the fifties would be incomplete without a discussion of hot wheels. Cue FERRARA:

What you see today in the design of automobiles is a continuation of what we as car owners were doing in our day, such as removing the ornaments and chrome from our cars. I was in a hot rod club, and we did all of our own work on cars. I used to know all the parts of an engine and how to fix one.

This club was made up of kids in the neighborhood. We would take the chrome off, fill in the holes, cover them with primer, and then paint them. We just loved working on cars, and we could make cars faster by putting extra carburetors on them or larger manifolds.

One of the things we could do to increase the horsepower was called "glass-packing." Basically, what you had was a muffler without all the baffling in it. It had Fiberglas packing and a muffled roar to it. The pipes came straight through the Fiberglas packing, and so there wasn't the sound bouncing back and forth. When you put baffling in the muffler, it runs quiet but also creates back pressure because the gases can't escape as easily. With the lake pipes we used, the gases could escape and the engine could breathe better and ran more efficiently, and that gave you more horsepower out of the same engine. Lake pipes had a split in the exhaust system in front of the muffler, which allowed some flames to come out. You could pull a little switch that cut the exhaust so it wouldn't go through the muffler—it went straight out of pipes on the side of the car.

PURCELL HIGH SCHOOL CAVALIER

Staubach's senior photo.

The guys who won at drag strips were the guys who could afford to buy the big, fast cars. We really didn't have much respect for them because we built ours own, where they bought theirs. We had respect for the guys who built their own cars.

What you saw came straight out of the movie *American Graffiti*. I was sort of on both sides of what you saw in the movie, being pretty much a strait-laced guy in school by day, kind of like the Ron Howard character, and a hot rodder after school, kind of like the John Milner character with the white T-shirt. I don't remember what Howard's name in the movie was, but Suzanne Somers's being in the movie is what sticks out in my mind.

We even had our own popular deejay who was our version of Wolfman Jack. In fact, the guy is still here doing radio shows more than forty years later—Jim LaBarbara, "the Music Professor," who works with WGRR-FM, an "oldies" station in Cincinnati. We also had two other guys in town who did the televised after-school dance parties a la Dick Clark.

I kind of miss those days. I later became a cop in the traffic section, and I used to chase down those kids using the souped-up cars. I drove one of the big interceptors with the big engines and would chase the kids in their muscle cars at over a hundred miles an hour on the expressway. The cars we had were built by Detroit for the purpose of chasing down speeders. And there were a lot of muscle cars on the road in those days, such as the big Ford 409s and the Plymouth Barracudas. I don't remember Roger being a part of that. It was a time when everybody drove big, fast cars. I got to drive fast chasing the cars that were driving fast. I drove a

Plymouth Fury III with a 383 engine and the big four-barrel carburetor, and it would haul.

VINCE EYSOLDT *talks about being recruited in those days and how college guys misread Staubach:*

Roger and I both got recruited by a bunch of schools. During a recruiting visit in those days, you would be taken around by an upperclassman, and their idea of taking you out was to take you to a bar and go drinking and carousing. That was a total turnoff to Roger, and, of course, these guys didn't know that at all.

JIM HEISELMANN:

Even my relatives in Texas who never met Roger consider him one of their heroes. I didn't really know him all that well in high school, but he was a genuine A-plus person. When he walked down the hall between classes, others would look at him in awe. "There's Rog!" But he never had a big head about it. He was one of the most humble guys you could ever meet, considering how popular he was.

ANCHORS AWEIGH

*W*HERE ELSE, BUT ANNAPOLIS? Knowing what we know now, or knew even thirty years ago, it is almost unfathomable to picture Roger Staubach playing quarterback at the college level at any place other than the Naval Academy. That would be like taking the Captain out of Captain America.

The story by now is a familiar one: Great athlete, great guy goes to the Naval Academy, wins the Heisman Trophy while his upstart team competes for the national title, gets drafted by America's Team-to-be, fulfills a four-year hitch as a naval officer (including a stint in Vietnam), and returns after four years away from top-notch football to give it a go with the Dallas Cowboys. This could have been scripted by a Hollywood screenwriter creating a real-life Frank Merriwell or Chip Hilton.

Roger Staubach, Ensign America.

What if?

Imagine the alternative: Staubach instead chooses to go to Notre Dame, and he, not John Huarte, wins the Heisman Trophy in 1964 instead of in 1963. What if Staubach had stayed closer to home and followed Woody Hayes's siren call to go to Ohio State? Three yards and a cloud of dust? As much as Roger the Dodger loved to run with the ball, this couldn't have been what he had in mind. He would have been a square peg in a round hole in Columbus.

Numerous big-name schools recruited Staubach, and even baseball's Cleveland Indians showed some interest along the way, but Roger had already made up his mind and made a commitment. Annapolis it would be, preceded by a year at New Mexico Military Institute in UFO-visited Roswell, where he could bring his English grades up to Naval Academy snuff.

Life as a Midshipman offered more challenges than a season full of Minnesota Vikings blitzes, going well beyond the patriotic images of dress whites, spit-polished shoes, knot-tying, scabbarded sabers, and anchored boats bobbing in the chop of nearby Chesapeake Bay. It was a relentlessly tough life of regimentation, early morning wake-ups, countless formations, three square meals a day, ample PT, verbal onslaughts from upperclassmen, demerits, rules, and regulations. And that's even before he got into the brutal engineering-centered curriculum and a major-college football schedule that presented a steady diet of Notre Dames, Michigans, Pittsburghs, Southern Cals, Penn States, Minnesotas, and those always pesky "Chinese bandits" from West Point on the banks of the Hudson.

Roger Staubach didn't get a free pass from his plebe year, but he endured it. Many others failed or dropped out along the way because they couldn't, or wouldn't, hack it as a Middie. This was a weeding-out process much more unforgiving than those employed nowadays by college coaches who run off marginal players to make more scholarship room for incoming blue-chippers.

Annapolis prepared Staubach well for a tour in Vietnam as well as for his days as an aspiring quarterback under Admiral Tom Landry. At Navy, a young Staubach had to bide his time while biting his tongue and waiting for his chance to play.

When the opportunity came his way, he was ready; oh, was he ready. The scenario would repeat itself with the Cowboys beginning in 1969.

JOE BELLINO, *Navy's Heisman Trophy winner in 1960 and one of Staubach's plebe-year football coaches in 1961, offers some background on football at Annapolis prior to Staubach's arrival there:*

My last year was just a continuation of our success from our teams in the late fifties. We had a nice run of Navy teams for a number of years. They had once led the nation in defense during that time, had gone on to be a top-ten team. We were in a rebuilding mode my second and third years, but at the end of our junior year was when we really jelled, culminating in a big victory over Army in which I scored three touchdowns.

Back then, we only dressed thirty-three players, so we really needed only fifteen or sixteen blue-chip players to be competitive. We had to play both ways then, and I remember being in great shape that year, in large part because I lived on the fourth floor of our dorm and, because we weren't allowed to use the elevator, I had to climb four sets of stairs six or seven days a week. Physically, I was healthy.

Three weeks into our season, we go out to the University of Washington, which had an all-junior team that was ranked number one. It was a nationally televised game, fortunately, and we upset them 15-14. We became a Cinderella team and kept winning games.

Our coach, Wayne Hardin, believed that if you had a good runner on your team, you should feature the run, and that's what he did. I can remember every Monday after games: I would meet with him and the first thing he would ask me was "Are you hurt? Did you get hurt?" I would say, "No, I feel great." He would then proceed to tell me about several new plays he was putting in for the next game to be ready for the next opponent.

RICK FORZANO *was an assistant coach at Navy whose recruiting territory included Ohio and, therefore, Staubach:*

I went to Cincinnati Purcell to look at a center by the name of Jerry Momper. While I'm there, the coach there tells me about this kid who's a junior playing defense and who is going to be moved to quarterback. I went to see a basketball game in which Roger was playing and he scored twenty-something points.

I came back in the spring, and he was a great baseball player, too. In fact, he turned down a lucrative offer from the Cleveland Indians while he was at school in New Mexico. When Roger had still been in high school, I tried calling him every Wednesday night for the longest period of time, and he would keep telling me about how he wanted to go to Notre Dame. He said he wanted to be a priest, and so I said, "Well, we can put that course of study in at the Naval Academy."

When I told people back at the Naval Academy about this guy, they thought I was nuts. But he still wanted Notre Dame. When he told me that, I thought, *Oh, boy.* Well, it turns out that Notre Dame told him he's going to be a walk-on, because they were bringing in more quarterbacks and had already given up all of the scholarships. I called him sometime later, expecting that he was going to tell me that he was going to go to Notre Dame. But he said, "Coach, I'm not going to Notre Dame; I'm going to Purdue." I said, "Purdue? What are you talking about?" He said, "Yeah, my parents will be able to see me play, for one thing."

His dad was sick at the time; he had diabetes and ended up having to have part of a foot cut off. I immediately got on an airplane and flew to Cincinnati. You know, you gotta be kinda lucky in life. I said to him, "Roger, why don't you think about a year of prep school?" He said he had never thought about it, and his mom and dad kind of perked up at that. I said, "It's a military school, and you'll find out if you like the military, and it'll give you a chance to bring up your grades (English, in particular)." Not that his grades were bad or anything; they just weren't quite good enough to get into the Naval Academy.

Out of high school, Roger had been selected to play in the state all-star game. Then coach of Roger's team had his nephew playing quarterback, so Roger was played as a wideout and defensive back. Roger made some tremendous catches, and on defense he came up and made a bunch of tackles. He even intercepted a pass. Then they put him in at quarterback and he led them in a comeback that almost won the game. By this time, everybody wants Roger.

I went into the locker room, and there were guys from a bunch of colleges all around him. Roger looked over at me and said, loud enough for everyone to hear, "Coach, I told you that I'm going to New Mexico. I'll be there." I said, "That's all I can ask, Roger." That's the type of guy he was, even then. You know they called him "Straight Arrow" at the Naval Academy. One time we were having a lackluster practice, and he got into the huddle and said, "Dammit!" Everybody just about fell over, but we went on to have a great practice.

Earlier, I had called the guy who was the football coach at the New Mexico Military Institute, Bob Shaw, who had been a great professional football player, to talk to him about Roger. He said, "Rick, I'm out of scholarships." I told him, "Let me tell you something. This guy will make you a great coach." Bob managed to scrounge up another scholarship for Roger, and the rest is history.

Roswell, New Mexico, is not the showplace for the world. It was just sand and more sand. Roger was as homesick as homesick can be. I would keep calling him and say, "Just hang in there, baby, and try another day." At the time, they were just in practice for the football season, and that can be really tough.

WAYNE HARDIN was the head coach at Navy at the time. He talks about how Forzano sold him and the rest of the coaching staff on that Staubach kid:

Rick kept coming back to school and telling us about this guy named Staubach, saying he was a heckuva player. Rick was building him up, building him up, building him up, and finally, I said, "Well, we gotta get him." Then Roger played in Ohio's North-South All-Star game, and Rick comes back and tells us, "You won't believe it, but Roger won both Outstanding Player on Offense and Outstanding Player on Defense." I said, "You're kidding," and Rick said, "No, that's the way it is, Coach."

Roger then spent that one year at New Mexico Military Institute, where they just kept winning and winning. It turns out that New Mexico is part high school and part postgraduate. The kids there who were still in high school were the officers, and the guys who were postgraduates were subservient to them. So these younger guys were calling the shots and making life miserable for these older guys, like Roger. So I called the coach down there (Bob Shaw), and he told me there wasn't a lot he could do about this. I asked him if there was anything he could do to help cut these guys at least a little slack. One thing about Roger is that he had a great sense of humor. So he and some other older guys finally took some of these younger guys, stuffed them into a barrel, and rolled them down the hill. Things leveled out after that.

RICK FORZANO:

One of the reasons we were able to get guys like Tom Lynch, Pat Donnelly, and Roger Staubach is that the Big Ten was on the confidential-need statement, and those guys would have had to pay money to go to those schools. Not that their parents didn't have much money, but they had enough money so that they could not get any aid. Ohio State could not have given Roger a full ride because of that. His parents both worked. That rule killed Big Ten football for five years—other schools were knocking them off (in recruiting) by telling some great blue-chippers that their parents would have to pay a thousand dollars a year to go to a Big Ten school.

STEVE BELICHECK, *whose son Bill coached the New England Patriots to the Super Bowl title after the 2001 season, was an assistant coach at Annapolis for more than thirty years, and knows better than just about anyone what it takes to successfully recruit a blue-chip athlete to a service academy:*

I enjoyed recruiting for the Naval Academy because it had so much more to offer than a civilian school. I would ask high school recruits, "After you graduate four years from now, what are you going to do? I'll tell you what you're going to do—you're going to have a job that's going to pay you a good wage. You're going to get further training in whatever field you go into, and you're going to get responsibility from the day that you get your first assignment. You are in a position to look around, should you eventually decide that the navy or the marines isn't something you want to spend a lifetime on, and see everything else that is available."

We also played a great schedule back then. Notre Dame, as always, was on our schedule every year, but we were also playing schools like Penn State, Pitt, Michigan, Southern Cal, Washington, Stanford, Boston College, Georgia Tech, Oklahoma, SMU, North Carolina, and Miami. That sounds really tough, yet we felt we could compete every week with those teams because, in the first place, we were in better shape than they were.

Throughout the fifties and early sixties, we knew we had plenty of players at Navy who could also play for any of those other schools. That's how good our talent base was. And I'm not talking just one or two guys. When the Vietnam War came along, it affected us, but not as much as it did Army. One thing you may not have heard much about was that there were congressmen, with their allotment to give out service academy appointments, who were taking money from well-to-do families who didn't want their sons to go to Vietnam and get shot. They could go to a service academy and during those four years be protected from having to serve in Vietnam. Many people thought the war would be over in less than four years, and so this sounded like a great way to be protected. Plus you got a great education in the process.

I made it a point when recruiting to talk to the parents. I would ask them, "Do you want your son going to the Naval Academy or to the University of Florida? If he goes to Florida, he could get drafted tomorrow and be over in Vietnam in nine months. If you go to the Naval Academy, there's no chance of your going over there for at least four years."

TOM LYNCH *was a year ahead of Staubach at the Naval Academy, where he played center and linebacker and was captain of the 1963 team that, in Staubach's junior year, went 9-1. Lynch later served as the superintendent at the Naval Academy from 1991 to 1994, before retiring from the navy in 1995. Lynch recently went to work for the Staubach Company:*

Freshmen didn't play varsity football in the sixties. When I was a sophomore (1961), Roger as a plebe was assigned to my company. It was a bad-news company as far as plebes go. The year before they had moved the second class around, which was my plebe year, and there had been a company called "the Terrible Tenth." If you were a plebe you did whatever you could to avoid going in the area of the Tenth Company because 50 percent of them got forced out of the Naval Academy.

These guys were the Bad News Bears. Those guys came over to my company, the Sixteenth Company, when I was a plebe, but our saving grace is that the first class of guys, the seniors, were more easygoing and not hard-assing the plebes all the time. So there was a little bit of a balance there; they couldn't go hog-wild. When those guys got to be seniors the next year, they wanted to make sure that everyone got a plebe year. If you were an athlete having privileges such as being able to eat meals at the team table, then you were a skater, a slacker, somebody that needed special attention. It was, Welcome to the Naval Academy, Roger.

BO COPPEDGE, Navy's athletic director from 1968 to 1988, became a Staubach acquaintance over the years. He expands on Lynch's assessment of life as a Midshipman at Annapolis:

There's no such thing as cutting class. If you do, you get put on report. You don't even think about doing that. There may be days that you feel like sleeping in in the morning, but that's not going to happen at Annapolis. You get up at 0615, are in formation by 0700, and then you march to breakfast. You then have until 0755 to eat your breakfast, get your room straight, and get to your first class.

Then there are all the little things that go with being a Midshipman. If you are a defensive tackle, for example, and you weigh 275 pounds, the chances of your going over and completing that rope climb are pretty narrow. You're going to end up having to do some things in P.E. class to get in shape to be able to do that, and that's in addition to all that you have to go through with football training, practice, and the games. That's the kind of thing you need to worry about.

On top of all that are the academics, and the curriculum is tough. All students, even the student-athletes, have to take a full load of classes all year round. Unlike at other schools, making up classes during the summer isn't that easy because there are always other obligations related to being a Midshipman that need to be taken care of. They don't get the summer off.

What you end up finding is that your mind can adjust to about anything, especially when you have to do it. You learn how to adjust to things like getting up at 0615 every morning, dressing quickly, and studying quickly and with plenty of focus at night. One break that football players get is that they didn't have to be back in uniform for the evening meal following practice.

ROGER STAUBACH *was not the perfect Midshipman. He racked up more than a hundred demerits in his plebe year, many of them while engaged in a year-long run-in with a first-class (senior) student, who went out of his way to make the football-playing plebe's first year as miserable as he could:*

I wasn't a wild kid at all, but the year at Roswell (at the New Mexico Military Institute) helped me adapt to military life. I had some trouble getting used to things like shining my shoes every day. I had priorities in my life, and shining my shoes hadn't been among them.

I also had some challenging times at Annapolis. The company I was in during my plebe year at the Naval Academy, Sixteenth Company, really didn't like the idea that I was able to eat on the training table, and I went from football to basketball to baseball. They kind of took it out on me in the hall, so I had some adjusting to do there as well. Polishing my brass, shining my shoes. I actually got quite a few demerits during my first six months, more than in my next three and a half years total. To work those off, there was different stuff I had to do, like walking the Yard or doing things on the weekend.

One thing I had to do as a plebe was go around to this guy's (an upperclassman's) room all the time—a guy by the name of Dave Borland—to do pushups, sit-ups, and this thing they called shoving out against the wall. I also had to memorize a bunch of stuff. He kind of took it upon himself to make sure I had a genuine plebe year at the Naval Academy. There were a few guys like that in the company, and they didn't ease up on me because I was an athlete. At least I was able to get away from some of the stuff by eating at the training table.

I got homesick a whole lot, mostly at Roswell the year before. I remember thinking a lot about leaving the school to go home. I was an only child, and my dad had been sick (diabetes) and wasn't doing well while I was in high school. My mother worked at

General Motors, and she was really happy about my going to the Naval Academy. She really wanted me to give it a shot and to go off and experience life beyond Ohio. If she hadn't encouraged me that way, I might have ended up back at the University of Cincinnati, which is where a lot of my buddies from high school went. But she wanted me to see the world a little bit.

I tried to do it all. I was a good student, graduating in the middle of my class. It was an engineering school, and some of my classes I did well in and some I didn't. I enjoyed the idea of having a balanced life, and this was a place that forced you to get a good education. I really wanted to also play baseball in college, and I was able to do both at Navy.

The military life helped me a lot in developing discipline, which is important in business. I was proud to graduate from the Naval Academy and be in a class with guys sharing such a common denominator. A lot of them went on to become naval heroes and I was fortunate to become a sports hero of sorts. Going to the Naval Academy was one of the best things that ever happened to me, even if I didn't make a career out of the navy. If I had it to do over again, I would do it the same way.

TOM LYNCH:

You've got to understand coming in to the Naval Academy that you are a Midshipman who happens to play football. You're not just going from high school to college, which is a pretty good transition in itself, but you're also going from civilian life to military—big transition. Then on top of that you go from being big man on campus and king of the prom to the bottom of the heap. You are a plebe.

At the Naval Academy you quickly surmise that everything you do in life you are going to have to accomplish on your own merit—you *personally*. It's not who your dad is; it's not what the color of your skin is; it's not who you know. It is all about *you* and nothing else.

So the first thing you are told to do is put away all the accouterments like any form of jewelry—you can't have a radio, you can't watch TV, and you've got to get a haircut, a buzz-cut, that is just like the other twelve or fourteen hundred guys in your class, and you're all going to wear the same uniform and learn how to salute.

You're going to change your normal pattern of life: You don't *walk* from one place to another—you're either marching or double-timing. If you see anybody who's senior to you, you always address them with "Good morning, sir" or "Good afternoon, sir." And if you're asked something, the only acceptable responses are "Yes, sir," "No, sir," or "I'll find out, sir." You're being prepared for a position of leadership, and leadership can be lonely, especially if you're in combat and you're going to have to make decisions while thinking on your feet and reacting under pressure. They start that with you from day one at the Naval Academy.

Adds LYNCH:

As a plebe you go through an entire year of formations and three squares a day. You march to the mess hall and, whether you're hungry or not, you sit there at that table. And there are certain rites—not to be confused with *rights*—that go with being a plebe. You will know every day the exact number of days left to graduation or until Christmas, and what movies are being shown in town, and who's starring in those movies. You will memorize not only the current menu at the mess hall, but the next one as well. So, a senior Midshipman comes up to you and says, "Midshipman Towle, sound off!! How many days are there until Christmas? (or) What's in *The New York Times* today?" If you don't know the answers, you're considered lazy, a slacker. You don't necessarily get demerits, but what does happen is you call attention to yourself, and that isn't what you want to do.

You also have this little book you are supposed to carry around with you that contains a whole bunch of information referred to as "brief points." It's got all kinds of history about the navy. These older guys use the information in there to put pressure on you. "Tell me about John Paul Jones." "What are all the monuments in the Yard, and what do they stand for?" To know all this stuff and to be ready to answer anything, you're up at five in the morning. It makes for a very long day, and these guys can just drive you right out of the Naval Academy if you can't handle it.

Roger was singled out because he was a football player. But they couldn't really get to him; the pressure never really got him down even though he had a pretty tough plebe year, really getting worked over. He couldn't just get through this by hauling off and smacking someone or by telling them to go jump in the lake: You had to get through plebe year before you could even think about playing varsity football. You've got to remember there are three thousand upperclassmen and a little more than a thousand plebes. Once these upperclassmen find out that you don't give a damn or that you can't hack it, then they figure that "maybe you shouldn't be in the navy, and maybe you aren't the type of leader that we want to have." Eventually, you either shape up and fly right, or you go home.

Football was a big relief from all this. In the first place, you could vent your frustration out on the field by hitting somebody. Secondly, you had a group of guys going through the same sort of stuff that you were going through, and that helped with the bonding process on the team. During the season you were excused from Monday parade practice and then the actual Wednesday afternoon parades. We got out of those both during the fall and again in the spring when we had spring football.

Then after all this is said and done, you've got to be able to cut it academically, because if you don't pass, you've got a problem. When I was in school, you had to maintain at least a 2.5 grade point average on a 4.0 scale. If you didn't, you either got sent home or, at best, you were termed "a turnback," where they would let you come back in the next class and start everything all over again. It's not as tough now.

*There wasn't a lot of time to really make friends during plebe
year, but football offered an opportunity to at least make
acquaintances away from the hustle and bustle of plebe life.
One of Staubach's newest friends that year turned out to be
EDWARD "SKIP" ORR, who had been a star left-handed quarterback at Chaminade High School on Long Island, New York.
At first, Orr didn't know it, but his quarterbacking days were
pretty much done by the time he got to Annapolis, where he
gained a friend at the same time he was losing a position:*

I heard Roger's name the first day of plebe summer. The first day.
There were some football players in my company who had played
with Roger when he was at New Mexico Military Institute. In the
limited amount of time we had to talk with each other, that's what
these guys started talking about—this guy by the name of Roger
Staubach. This was the end of June, and football didn't start until
mid-August.

I'd be talking with these guys, and after we had talked a bit
about where we had played and so forth, some guy asked me what
position I played. When I said quarterback, the guys who had
played against Roger said to me, "Don't get your hopes up. You're
not going to play quarterback. There's this guy Roger Staubach
who's probably going to be the best quarterback Navy has ever
had." At that point, I start to think, *Hmmm, maybe I made the
wrong choice here.*

I think the first time Roger and I met was when we were playing baseball. In that period before football started, you had to play
another sport. We had both played baseball in high school, and I
could see that he also was a great, great baseball player. I think he
would have had a legitimate shot at playing in the major leagues.
He had a strong arm and was a good outfielder, and he could hit.

At the start of baseball, we were going through tryouts, and he
was playing center while I played right. We kind of latched on to
each other as friends. Other than the great disparity in our football

talents, we had a lot of things in common. We had both gone to all-boys Catholic schools and played the same three sports. We were both pretty religious guys, and we both were dating our high school sweethearts. We even had similar builds, and with our short haircuts, we sometimes were confused for one another when in uniform. A couple of weeks into baseball, or about a month before the start of football, he asked me if I wanted to go throw the football around a little bit so we could start getting ready for football season. I said sure. The first time I saw him throwing a football, I knew that being quarterback wasn't going to happen for me.

ORR talks more about that year of plebe football, which saw the young Middies go 9-1 with Staubach at the helm, losing only to the Maryland freshmen:

Plebes, being freshmen, weren't allowed to play varsity football in those days, and anybody could try out for plebe football. On the first day of practice, we had twenty-two quarterbacks going out. Joe Bellino, the 1960 Heisman Trophy winner from Navy, was one of our coaches.

I can remember a couple of impressions from that first day. One, *Let's hope I can be number two* (behind Staubach). That's as good as I was going to be able to do. Two, *I was just in awe of Joe Bellino.* He had just graduated. There he was in T-shirt and shorts, and this was the most muscular guy I had ever seen. And just a super guy.

I just kind of gutted it out, playing second team part of the year and third team part of the year. I was still playing quarterback the following spring, but after spring practice the coaches came to me and said, "Let's look at reality here. You're not going to play quarterback at Navy, but you've got athletic ability. Why don't you see about trying it at wide receiver?" Actually, we called it flanker. So that's what I did, even though I had never played any position other than quarterback.

After winning the Heisman in 1960 as a senior at Navy,
JOE BELLINO graduated in the spring of 1961 and then stayed
on at Annapolis for about six months to help out with the
plebe football team. This was before Bellino spent two years
on a destroyer based at Norfolk, after which he went to
minesweeping school and then served aboard a minesweeper
in the South China Sea. Bellino:

Actually, I did see Roger play at Navy as a plebe because I was his backfield coach. That's because I had remained at the Academy and helped with coaching and recruiting for the six months between my graduation and commissioning.

Roger obviously had the talent to move out of the pocket, make the right decision, and throw. At the end of the plebe year, all the coaches got together to evaluate the team, and Wayne Hardin had Roger slated to be a *halfback.* I, along with the head plebe coach, vehemently opposed that and said, "This guy is a quarterback." Selfishly, I have told Roger over the years that "I was the key guy in keeping you at quarterback. They wanted to put you at halfback. I'm glad they listened to me, because if they had put you at halfback, you would have broken my records."

As a matter of fact, I sent Roger a photograph that accompanied an article that *Sport* magazine did on me concerning my year after winning the Heisman. The photo showed me in a group with young quarterbacks, and I was showing them, including Roger, how to hold the ball. I later sent him the article with a note that said, "See, Roger, I made you." He got a kick out of it.

BELLINO, *on being a Middie:*

I found it easy. Most high school athletes that are blue-chippers and follow a routine are prepared for the Naval Academy and being under the gun on time management. Anyone who plays sports doesn't have a problem with that kind of regimentation. If you're footloose and fancy-free, it's hard following those kinds of rules. If you're an athlete, it's ideal.

Staubach's sterling reputation as a crack quarterback and team leader his plebe year made the rounds at Annapolis. There was a bit of the wise guy in him, too, as WAYNE HARDIN *recalls:*

When Roger came into his first varsity practice after the end of plebe season, we had picture day. Roger came over to me at one point and said, "Hey, Coach, why not just take a picture of all the starting plebes from last year because they're also going to be your starters next season anyway." He wasn't too far from wrong.

We didn't have much of a team in 1961, but we had a group of kids who demonstrated what could be done when enough effort was put forth. Our quarterback that year was Ron Klimeck, and he took us to a 7-3 season, and in the three games we lost (against Pittsburgh, Penn State, and Duke) we were heavy underdogs. That, I thought, was one of the great efforts from a team that was the underdog in almost every game.

After we had gotten through spring practice the following spring (1962), by my analysis Roger hadn't beaten Ron out for the starting quarterback position. That's why I started Ron, and he deserved the opportunity—that Roger had to show, clear-cut, that he was better than Ron before I would replace Ron with him.

The first time Roger got in a game was against Michigan, which had guys so big they were blocking out the sun. I put him in when we were back on the twenty-yard line, and on one play one of their guys picked Roger up by his facemask and then smacked him down to the ground. The next thing I know I'm in the middle of the field, and I'm not even sure how I got there. I was scared to death that Roger's neck had been broken. I was kneeling down beside Roger to make sure he was okay, when an official came over. I said, "It appears that he's okay, so I'll leave and you can just start penalizing these guys any time." We ended up getting beat, 21-0.

Another of Staubach's teammates all the way through their four years at Annapolis was PAT DONNELLY, *who, like Lynch and Orr, works for Staubach today:*

I met Roger toward the end of plebe summer at one of the early meetings for football players. Almost everybody who played high school football went out for the football team, so we had about five or six hundred, out of about twelve or thirteen hundred from the plebe class, showing up to play football. It was a huge turnout, and soon word got out as to who the super-recruits were. Roger had gone to military school for a year before coming, and his was one of the names we heard a lot. All that talk led to the assumption that he must be some sort of hotshot. But when you met him, you found out he was a regular guy—and he still is.

We hit it off pretty well from the beginning, in part probably because we were both from Ohio. We were in different companies that first year, so we didn't see that much of each other, but during the following summer we went on the same ship together for what was referred to as youngster cruise, referring to the third class—sophomores. We were both on an aircraft carrier, the USS *Forrestal*, which was home-ported in Norfolk, Virginia, and went up and down the East Coast. That lasted almost two months.

After plebe year was over, Staubach and his peers hit the seaways for their first extended cruise as Midshipmen, destination New York. DONNELLY:

On our youngster cruise between our freshman and sophomore years, we went up to New York City and went to a dance that had been arranged for us in a hotel ballroom. The procedure at these dances was that the sponsoring organization sent out invitations to young women at various schools. At the dance they would be brought in from one direction, and we were herded in from another direction, and we paired up as the two lines came together.

You could tell before you stopped if a good-looking girl would end up across from you. If there was a girl that guys were trying to avoid, you could feel the line being pushed back. When Roger got close to the front and got a glimpse of someone he thought he would like to meet, he pushed ahead of a couple of guys and managed to snag this one.

It turned out that her parents lived in northern New Jersey at one of the beach towns, and a bunch of us went out there the next day after Roger asked her if he could bring along some of his friends and if she could do the same. There were three or four of us. But after we got there, this girl really started putting a lot of pressure on Roger—she obviously liked him. He was getting uncomfortable with this, and he asked us to help him out. He wanted to ease out and the only way he could do that was by one of the other of us showing some interest in her.

So I volunteered, and she and I ended up going out a few times, and then the same thing happened to me. She seemed intent on having a long-term relationship with a Midshipman. After we got back to school, she wanted to come to the Naval Academy at every opportunity. By this time, we were in football season, and she would ask, "Well, what about next weekend?" And I said, "I don't have any plans for after the game, but we're playing down at Duke next weekend." I assumed there was no way she would be interested, but she said, "Okay, I'm coming."

I ended up doing the same thing Roger had, introducing her to another guy. She was okay with that. And no, her name wasn't Debra Winger (who co-starred with Richard Gere in *An Officer and a Gentleman*). She was a lot closer to West Point, but maybe she had already tried that route.

Life aboard a ship at sea wasn't exactly all exhilaration for the youngsters, as DONNELLY *points out:*

We weren't given a lot of responsibility on cruises, not having any particular skills. It was mostly labor-type work such as swabbing decks and chipping paint. The main focus was learning some basic instruction and how to take orders. We also spent some time at the ship's helm, sometimes being allowed to work the steering.

Our youngster cruise went pretty well in terms of our not getting too seasick. As an aircraft carrier, the *Forrestal* was pretty big, and so it didn't roll very much. But during our first-class cruise, during the summer between our junior and senior years, we were in the Mediterranean on a guided-missile frigate, and Roger was deathly seasick for about the first week. He couldn't function and could barely get out of bed. As long as he was horizontal and in bed, he wasn't too sick. It started wearing off after four or five days. I think there were a few guys who feigned seasickness so they could get out of some duties and stay in bed, but that wasn't Roger. It wasn't an act.

If you want to meet a trivia expert and historian when it comes to football at the service academies, start with writer and author JACK CLARY, *who offers these scattershot tidbits about Staubach at the Naval Academy:*

Roger was an altar boy at the Naval Academy. He went to Mass several times during the week, even with the schedule he had, and the priest he served, a former football player, was a naval hero as a chaplain who went on to win the Legion of Merit. When the priest was passing away, Roger made several trips to visit him on his deathbed.

Roger was a hero in the brigade, a genuine hero. Guys would stop him and ask for his autograph. Members of the brigade showed their admiration by giving Roger a gift of blue and gold rosary beads. Those were the colors for the Navy football team and for the Virgin Mary, to whom the rosary is dedicated. It was the first and only time that the brigade so honored one of its own.

Roger finished his four years with a GPA of between 2.9 and 3.0, so he was in the middle of his class with about a B average. He did have his problems with courses such as mechanical drawing and metallurgy. Electrical engineering was probably a problem for him, too, because it was for everybody else. Why should he be any different?

In basketball Staubach held Army's leading scorer to six points in the first half, and he sat out the second half. Staubach didn't score, but Navy upset Army, 55-48. After the game Major General William C. Westmoreland, then the superintendent of West Point, sought out Ben Carnevale, the basketball coach at Navy, and said, "Dammit, Carnevale, Staubach's no basketball player," and Carnevale said, "No, sir, but he is a winner."

BILL BUSIK, *now retired but still living in Annapolis, was the Naval Academy's athletic director when Staubach arrived. Staubach was promoted to the varsity in 1962 as a sophomore, although, as would be the case seven years later with the Dallas Cowboys, Staubach found himself highly touted and yet cooling his heels behind the starting quarterback:*

We had had a so-so season in 1962. We had a little trouble with morale and some other things that I'd rather not go into, but there were just a lot of things that had to be cleaned up. Roger was sitting there not being played. The coach (Wayne Hardin) wanted a dropback quarterback and Roger, of course, was Roger the Dodger. It turns out that halfway through the season, when we weren't doing well, the starting quarterback (Ron Klimeck) got hurt. It was in the Cornell game that Roger came in to take the other quarterback's place, and we ended up blowing them out, 41-0. For the rest of the year, Roger was the regular quarterback and we beat Army, so it was obvious that everything was turning around.

TOM LYNCH *explains how that so-so 1962 season set up what would be a spectacular 1963 season, both from a team standpoint and from Staubach's perspective:*

The Naval Academy team of 1963 really was a special group of guys who had a strong bond. And it was a strong bond long before we finished 9-1 or Roger won the Heisman.

I'm really not sure what happened to create that, only that it was a confluence of a lot of things. One, as freshmen, those of us who had been there in 1960 saw that a Navy team could be top three in the nation. Two, when no one predicted we would have much, in 1961, we were tough and scrappy and won some games that we probably shouldn't have, and we wound up 7-3. Then, in 1962, we had a little bit of complacency as a team because we knew we had a lot of talent. We had even talked about it on summer cruise, saying things like, "Hey, I wonder if we'll go to the Sugar Bowl or if maybe we should aim for the Cotton Bowl. Which one do we want to go to this year?" We had the kind of attitude that all we had to do was toss our jocks out onto the field and we would win, and as any experienced coach will tell you, that's when you get your jock handed to you. The next thing we knew, we had gotten knocked on our butts.

Late in the season we played Southern Cal in Los Angeles at the Coliseum, and they were ranked number one. We really should have won that ball game, losing 13-6. Pat Donnelly, who hardly ever fumbled, lost the ball while crossing the goal line, and it was ruled that he fumbled it before getting into the end zone.

U.S. NAVAL ACADEMY, STU WHELAN

Navy's 1962 team photo, when Staubach was a sophomore. That's Staubach in the fourth row on the far right, wearing No. 12. Among his close friends in the photo is Pat Donnelly, No. 38 in the back row, almost right behind Staubach.

We just couldn't quite put it away. Then we had two weeks off and killed Army, 34-14. That was the springboard, the finish that gave us the confidence going into the next season.

Staubach's quarterbacking predecessor, Ron Klimeck, was a big kid with a strong arm, a classic dropback passer. Staubach had a good arm, but he had the edge over Klimeck in two other areas—his uncanny running and scrambling ability, and the intangible of being able to convince his teammates in a huddle that they could accomplish whatever they set out to do.
TOM LYNCH:

Klimeck was a dropback, in-the-pocket passer. We didn't change things drastically when Roger got settled in at quarterback, except perhaps for a few more plays such as quarterback draws. A lot of it was just Roger taking off—these were not designed plays. I can remember after each game telling myself that there is nothing else that Roger can do that would surprise me, and then we would play another game and he would do something else that surprised me.

One game in particular was when we played Duke. I think it was down in Norfolk. The first half of the game was pretty much all back and forth. Then right before the half, Roger pulled off another one of his amazing plays.

We had a play that we sometimes used with some success where Roger would fake the draw to the fullback, drop back, jump up in the air, twist in the air, and flip the ball out to the halfback in the flat for a screen pass. Right before the half in that Duke game, we ran the play and there were three guys coming right in on Roger and they also had the halfback covered out in the flat. So this time, when Roger jumped up in the air, he held on to the ball, came down, shook loose from the defenders, and took off, all the way down the field, cutting around strewn bodies, for the touchdown. You can't coach that kind of play.

SKIP ORR *was still on the junior varsity his sophomore year when Staubach was in the process of replacing Klimeck at quarterback. Orr knew what was happening, even if he wasn't always right there to see it:*

Ron was a strong guy and a real good guy, too. But everybody knew that one week it was going to happen, that we were going to be able to see Staubach in there. The only question was, When's the coach going to make the move?

The team wasn't reaching its total potential. Then came the Cornell game, when Roger got put in in place of Klimeck and took total control of the game, scrambling, running, throwing the ball—all the same things he had done as a plebe. Not that Cornell is Michigan, but he did have an unbelievable day.

I remember watching the Saturday afternoon NCAA football reports that day that detailed all he had done (Orr wasn't yet on the varsity team), and that was when the media first got word there was this really exciting sophomore quarterback at the Naval Academy. What a great story! America could really relate to the service academies, and here was a guy good enough to have played anywhere.

STEVE BELICHECK:

Roger had a remarkable knack about him in being able to sense pressure that he couldn't see, coming from the back side. He would take off and run away from trouble. It's not often that you see tall, lanky guys with long strides being able to scramble that well, but Roger was that rare exception. He was kind of like (Joe) DiMaggio in that regard—he could really run fast even though it didn't look like he was. A lot of guys going after him thought they had an angle on him, but when they got there, Roger wasn't there.

Where BILL BUSIK *had found himself having to light a match under the football squad in 1962, he discovered in 1963 that his need to be a disciplinarian had not diminished:*

Before the 1963 season, I had to straighten some things out. We had moved our preseason training camp from Rhode Island back to Annapolis to keep things a bit more disciplined, but even then we had gotten some report slips coming. Some of the players had been doing things they weren't supposed to be doing, such as playing around with the elevator in the building in which they stayed. It was off-limits. They were supposed to be using the stairs. The elevator was for workers to use when they had to move stuff up or down in the building. The commandant found out about this and told me that I needed to meet with these guys and get things straightened out.

When I got them together, I said, "Now, gents, you've had a few little skirmishes here, and I've got permission from the commandant that, if you have a reasonable excuse for doing these things, I can forgive you. You all have done pretty good on most of the occasions, but there's one guy here that I question. Just one guy. So, Roger Staubach, what do you have to say for yourself?"

You should have seen him. He was looking all around, as if to say, "What's going on here?" I said, "Now this report says that you not only went up in the elevator but that you also went down in the elevator. And your excuse was that what went up had to come down." The whole place just broke up, but Roger was real serious and yelled out, "I didn't say that, Captain!" Anyway, we got a big laugh out of it.

BUDD THALMAN, *Navy's twentysomething public relations director at the time, offers his take on what was transpiring in 1963 and how he jumped on the Staubach bandwagon early on:*

You can't talk about '63 without starting with the '62 season. Roger was absolutely phenomenal in the 34-14 victory over Army to end the season, passing for two touchdowns and running for two more. He did everything known to man: He was all over the field running, throwing the ball, scoring touchdowns.

He had been playing well for about seven weeks. In our first three games, he had played a total of something like seven minutes and thrown four incomplete passes. I don't know what Wayne (Hardin) was waiting for because Roger had been sensational as a plebe. From the time he finally got into the lineup against Cornell in the fourth game of the year, he played really well.

At the beginning of the '63 season, I put together this four-page brochure, about the size of a post card, titled "Meet Roger Staubach." Remember, in those days there was no ESPN and the only television coverage we got was the Army-Navy game at the end of the season. On the inside of the brochure were two pages of statistics about Roger as well as what I had written for the press guide, and on the back page I put some quotes from people talking about Roger and his '62 season. I put this brochure in all my preseason mailings to media.

A couple of years ago I was talking to Bill Rhoden of *The New York Times*, who was working on a piece about Heisman hype and what schools do in the form of CDs, Web sites, videos, and all that kind of stuff. It's unbelievable what is now being done. While interviewing me, Bill finally says, "As far as I can tell, you are the Father of Heisman Hype." I said, "Oh, that's a *real* distinction."

THALMAN *continues:*

The most interesting thing that happened in 1963 was a conversation I had with Wayne Hardin before the season. He said, "We should really go all out this season for Roger to win the Heisman Trophy. You should go to New York every Monday for the New York writers' luncheon in Manhattan." In 1963 New York was the center of the universe, and that's where all the wire services were based, where the television networks were headquartered, and they had six to eight newspapers in town in those days. So on every Monday during the '63 season, I boarded a train in Baltimore, went to the writers' luncheon in New York, and came back on the same day.

I had worked all day Sunday, the previous day, to put together all of Roger's updated stats and some quotes from the game, and would also take along a film clip from the Saturday game if I had one. That's the one thing I did that year that I thought was unique in promoting Roger's candidacy. It was Wayne's idea.

It also helped that Roger was playing just unbelievably well. I mean, the first three games of the season he was just lights out. We played Michigan in the third week and he had a game for the ages, gaining 307 total yards. If there was a moment where he won

Staubach scrambling against Michigan in 1963 on his way to racking up 307 total yards and taking another big step toward the Heisman Trophy.

the Heisman Trophy, I always thought it was that play against Michigan in which he scrambled at least twenty-five yards behind the line of scrimmage, got hit by several players, and, while going down parallel to the ground, completed the pass to Pat Donnelly that resulted in the short gain of a yard or two. That was a big stage in the Big Ten Conference in a show-me game before more than a hundred thousand people.

TOM LYNCH, *by now a senior, saw the 1963 season as his class's last chance to make an everlasting impact on Navy football:*

The next year, 1963, we as seniors decided that we would make damn sure that we provided the right example and leadership to the rest of the team. We were going to make sure that no one ever got complacent. You do that by always hustling on practice days, and when you hit you hit hard. You just keep the intensity and the drive, and make sure the sophomores and juniors see what you are doing. As a result, we finished up 9-1 going into the Cotton Bowl, and we should even have been 10-0. But we lost to SMU, 32-28.

I remember seeing films of our SMU game afterwards and watching this one long pass play right before the half where one of our guys got called for pass interference. The film shows that our guy was never within five yards of the receiver at any point during the play. I was told that one Southwest Conference official got fired and that one or two others got put on probation after that game. And that pass-interference call was just one of the questionable calls in the game.

That whole weekend was kind of strange, as it turned out, because we played SMU on a Friday night and stayed over in Dallas the next day to watch the Texas-Oklahoma game at the Cotton Bowl. There might not even have been one pass thrown in that game, and then we end up after the season playing Texas at the same stadium, the Cotton Bowl, and losing because they were able to throw on us so well.

What I remember most about that trip is after our game with SMU on Friday night. Our normal routine at the Naval Academy was to play a game on Saturday, take Sunday off, have a light workout in sweats on Monday and then go over to the boathouse, where Coach Hardin would go through the film of Saturday's game one time and maybe point out a few things. Then we would go to an adjoining room and have a team dinner. Then it was back to the film room, where Steve Belicheck would give us a chalk talk regarding our next opponent. Then it was back on a bus and back to Bancroft Hall so we could begin studying by 7:15. That was our routine.

Coach Hardin always wore a green felt hat, his good-luck hat, at ball games to go with his coat and tie. We opened the season against West Virginia and won 51-7. That Monday he called us together and took off his hat, and inside the liner, engraved in gold, was "WVA." The next week we played William and Mary, and he's got "WMN" engraved in the hat's liner. Third game of the season, we go out to Michigan and beat their butt—they had eleven guys that had to be carried off the field—and on Monday afternoon, following our light workout, he showed us "MICH" engraved in gold. So far so good.

Then we play at SMU and get beat, 32-28. A lot of bad officiating, all one way. On Monday, Coach Hardin calls us together and we're all saying, "What's he going to do now? We're going to love this one." He takes off his hat and shows us the liner, and this time it says "SBT." SBT? "Screwed, blued, and tattooed," he says. That was Hardin for you; he was great.

Head coach WAYNE HARDIN *said he had been tipped off by an unlikely expert source that he had a national-title contender on his hands long before the season even started:*

During spring practice in 1963, I was driving home one night when I decided to stop at a butcher's shop on the way. I went inside to get some meat, and this was a guy I knew because I bought meat there every now and then. He says to me, "Coach, I've got everything figured out." I said, "Okay. Tell me, would ya?"

"You guys are going to be undefeated and be number one in the country next year."

"Okay, what are you smoking?"

"No, really! I've studied the schedule and every player, and I know what you guys are going to do. You're going to be number one."

A little later I called the team together and told them, "Gentlemen, my butcher tells me that you're going to be number one in the country. I believe him, and I want you to believe it, too. So let's go to work on it."

HARDIN *describes what added dimensions Staubach brought to the team in 1963, now that he was clearly the number-one quarterback:*

Roger brought individual talent to a team that needed help. We didn't win a lot of games that first year with him at quarterback—he won his first three but then lost the next three. But what he brought into the team was incredible . . . excitable. At one point after Roger had taken over, one of the other coaches said, "Hey, why don't we put in the quarterback draw?" And I said, "Why screw things up? We've already got it."

"What do you mean we've got it."

I said, "Staubach drops back to run, not to pass."

He'd see a crack and was gone, and that wasn't in the play-book. I didn't want to do anything to destroy that.

One play we did put in for him was a rollout in which he would go nine yards to one side and then decide whether to take off running or throw. Sometimes if he didn't see anything he liked on that side, he would take off in the other direction and go all the way to the other side of the field. The coaches would start to say something about it, and I would say, "Leave it alone. I like to watch him." Heck, I didn't know what was going to happen next, and I wanted to find out. It was like reading a good story—you want to read the ending for yourself.

We'd tell the linemen, "Look, you know when Roger's going to be rolling out to the side. Don't worry about sliding all the way down the line with him looking to pick up blocks. Just wait around because you know Roger is going to be coming back through, and when he comes back then you can level those guys." Time after time after time that's what happened. After a while, guys got the feeling that everything was going to work out, and it did. I mean, Roger was a heckuva runner.

HARDIN *elaborates on Staubach, the runner and scrambler:*

Roger was really a rawboned cowboy. He could have punched cattle; he could have done anything, really.

When people would say to me that Roger was doing too much

of that running-around stuff, I would say, "Leave him alone. I know it's going to come out okay." And it always did. He didn't choke up the ball, fumble it, or throw interceptions (much). He didn't do stupid stuff. The only think he was thinking out there while running the ball all over the place was, *"All I want to do is get this damn ball into the end zone."*

I remember a time when we played Michigan and at one point had the ball down on around their five- or six-yard line. Rog goes back to pass, doesn't like what he sees, reverses his field a little bit left, gets hemmed in, reverses it to the right, gives up some ground. . . . After a while he passes me out by the fifty-yard line, and he's still running around the ball. I'm standing there thinking, *I wonder what he's going to do now?* All of a sudden, a few defensive guys get him surrounded, lift him up off the ground, and he's now parallel to the field. He throws a sidearm pass to Pat Donnelly, and Pat takes it back for a one-yard gain. How can you get mad at a guy like that?

By the time the 1963 season started, the Legend of Roger Staubach was sweeping America. It even touched former high school classmates in Cincinnati, such as Gene Ferrara:

I was a football fan and went to some of Navy's games, such as the 1963 game at Michigan (which Navy won, 26-13, to improve to 3-0). I remember parking in a guy's front lawn, and it was awesome seeing Roger and Navy beat Michigan, let alone to be sitting in a stadium that sat 105,000 people. We had to walk about a mile and a half to get to the stadium.

Three weeks later, after a loss to SMU in the interim, Navy took on the undefeated Pittsburgh Panthers in a showdown for Eastern supremacy. Pat Donnelly:

We were ranked around tenth and Pittsburgh in the top two or three in the nation. And we beat them fairly decisively (24-12). I remember Jim Campbell's having an exceptional game receiving, and I also remember Tom Lynch's intercepting a pass in that game and lateraling the ball to me as he was about to get tackled on the return.

(U.S. NAVAL ACADEMY, NATE FINE)

Staubach, out of football uniform and into naval uniform, meets another young admirer among millions.

One of the games we struggled with was against VMI (Navy won, 21-12, the week before Pitt), which was a heavy underdog to us. We didn't win by much. We had a field goal partially blocked and everyone watched the ball dribble around in the end zone, and the only player on the field who realized it was still a live ball was our kicker, Fred Marlin. He went down into the end zone and recovered the ball for a touchdown. That was the key play in the game, but we won it and that kept us going.

Let's go back to that SMU game in the fourth week of the season, which the Midshipmen lost, 32-28, at the Cotton Bowl in Dallas. One person very familiar with that game, but who did not want to be identified while being interviewed for this book, insists that the published point spread of the game went from showing Navy as a fourteen-point favorite to even in a period of less than twenty-four hours right before the

start of the Friday night game. And, that source says, one of
the Southwest Conference officials that worked that game
was, allegedly, a known gambler. BILL BUSIK, who was not
the source for that allegation, has his own bad memories of
that SMU loss:

In 1963 we were undefeated and went down to Dallas to play
SMU. On one particular play, Roger handed the ball off and then
an SMU guy, who wasn't even listed on the game roster, came in
late and just decked him, dislocating Roger's shoulder. I can
remember seeing on the film the official right behind the play
reaching in his back pocket to throw a penalty flag, looking
around at the other officials to see if anyone else was going to
throw a flag, and then putting his back in his pocket. This kind of
thing was going on throughout the game.

Roger was taken to the dressing room and taped up after they
got his shoulder back in place, and he went back into the game
and damn near beat them anyway. In spite of that, we still were
number two in the country by the end of the year after we beat
Army to end the regular season. This was right after President
Kennedy had been assassinated in Dallas. The superintendent of
the Naval Academy at the time [Rear Admiral C. C. Kirkpatrick]
was a Texan, and I can remember his saying after the assassination
that the Naval Academy would never play another game in Texas.
Well, there I was with a contract in my pocket committing us to
play Texas in the Cotton Bowl, if we beat Army. In those days, you
had to beat Army to play in a bowl game.

I got called up to his office to meet with the superintendent
and the commandant. The superintendent had heard how the
team still wanted to go to the Cotton Bowl, and he asked me why
I thought we should still go. I said, "Because we have made a con-
tractual commitment and the team wants to go."

"Who'd you ask?" the superintendent asked me.

"The captain of the team (Tom Lynch)."

Now this guy was a pretty feisty guy, and I can still see him
banging his fist on his desk and saying to me, "Is that your idea of

leadership? I want to see the captain of the team." He knocked a whole bunch of papers off his desk as he said this, and I could see the commandant sitting off to the side shivering.

The next morning at eight, I went back there with Tom (Lynch), and this is a perfect example of just how much a helluva leader Tom is. He gave a great talk to the superintendent about why we should still go to the game, showing the same kind of leadership that had been so instrumental in turning the team around between 1962 and 1963. Tom did a marvelous job in explaining how this Cotton Bowl game would be the last chance for these seniors—of which Tom was one—to play in a big game to cap what had perhaps been the greatest season in Naval Academy football history. After Tom got done speaking, the superintendent excused himself, went to a telephone, and called a newspaper reporter down in Texas to say, "Hey, forget everything I had said to you earlier about our not coming to Texas."

PAT DONNELLY:

The SMU game was kind of a strange game. I remember our being able to move the ball pretty well, but for some reason we were unable to stop them. I remember their band being on the sideline and harassing us, sometimes even physically getting in the way as some of us tried coming off the field or after we were involved in a play that went out of bounds. I had never seen that before—definitely a homefield advantage.

Okay, so Navy lost that game for its only regular-season loss of the 1963 season. One of those in attendance at the game was GIL BRANDT, *the Dallas Cowboys' always observant director of player personnel:*

Roger looked really, really good, and we knew some people at the Naval Academy. We ended up drafting him in the tenth round (in 1964) at about four in the morning.

In those days you had the AFL and the NFL, and it was an unwritten rule then that you didn't sign redshirts until after their complete college eligibility was finished. But you tried to protect your prey so to speak, and the way we protected them was during the summer I would spend three or four weeks visiting the guys we had drafted as redshirts. Roger, of course, was one of them. I flew to Cincinnati and got with his mom and dad, and this was while Roger was on cruise at the Naval Academy. I went out to dinner with his parents, and I can remember walking into their house and seeing crucifixes on the wall and so forth. They were a very religious family.

We had a great conversation. I got around to asking them if Roger had a girlfriend, and they said, "Oh, yeah, Marianne (Hoobler) has been his girlfriend since the fourth grade." I said, "Well, you know, if Roger were to get married, he wouldn't have to serve his time in the navy." I could not have said anything worse than that. It would have implied that somehow he wanted to get out of his service commitment. I almost screwed that deal up.

People never thought that much of Roger while he was in high school. He desperately wanted to go to Ohio State, according to Woody Hayes, and Ohio State did not recruit him high. Roger then had that great game in the Ohio North-South All-Star football game, and Woody tried to get back in there to convince Roger to go to Ohio State rather than go to the Naval Academy.

We also knew the guy who was the head football coach at the New Mexico Military Institute, a guy by the name of Bob Shaw. We called him and Bob told us that Roger was a tremendous person with great ability.

One thing we had always done a pretty good job of was cultivating basketball coaches. It just so happens that the Naval Academy had a basketball coach by the name of Danny Peterson, who had been the coach at Michigan State at a time when we had been recruiting some basketball players with skills that we thought would translate well to football. By the time Roger got to the Naval Academy, Danny was coaching basketball there, so we called and asked him to baby-sit Roger for us. And that's what he did, singing the praises of the Cowboys to Roger almost every day.

It was ironic that we were playing in Philadelphia the day after the Army-Navy game. That night after the game, a captain by the name of Paul Borden—who

U.S. NAVAL ACADEMY

Roger Staubach at the Naval Academy, with two of the many honors he received while there.

might have been their athletic director at one time—helped us consummate the deal with Roger, and we gave Roger a bonus ($10,000) even though we had no idea if he would ever come play football for us or not. After Roger got to Vietnam, I would get these letters from him asking me to send six more footballs or whatever, that he was practicing football with some guys not far from where some bombs had landed.

While he was in the service, Roger would schedule some of his R and R to meet up with us at our training camp in Thousand Oaks, California. He would come to all the practices and attend our meetings; the only difference was that instead of staying in a dorm room with the rest of the team, he would stay at a nearby hotel.

*Long before the Cowboys finally got their hands on Staubach,
he was still back in Annapolis taking charge and inspiring
teammates while even motivating a few to reach deeper
within themselves.* WAYNE HARDIN:

We had a really good running back named Johnny Sai whom we
had recruited out of California. He was what you would call laid-
back. I kept pushing him, but it didn't seem to help. I didn't usually like to run guys after practice because I liked to keep practices to an hour and a half, and I worked them hard for those
ninety minutes. But Roger took it upon himself to whip Johnny
Sai into shape.

Now, Johnny was a fast guy. He could run the hundred in 9.8.
So after practice, while in full football gear, Roger took Johnny
out to the track, just the two of them. Roger said to him, "Johnny,
I'm going to beat your butt out here. I'm going to outrun you in
the forty."

Johnny says, "You can't beat me."

Now, Roger wasn't slow, and Johnny had to run his best to
beat him. The first time, Johnny barely edged out Roger. But Roger
wouldn't quit; he kept pushing him and pushing him. They even
got to where they took off the pads and kept racing each other,
and Roger would do this every day after practice, just to get
Johnny into shape, while at the same time satisfying his own competitive urge.

I knew it worked when we played Duke that season. We were
ahead something like 27-21 at the half, and I was telling our guys
that it looked like we were going to have to score fifty or sixty
points to win, and I didn't think we could score that many, so I
told them that they had better play some defense in the second
half. And they did.

We started out with the ball in our end and couldn't get out.
We punted to Duke, and they couldn't get into our end of the
field. We couldn't get out, they couldn't get in; we couldn't get out,
they couldn't get in. Fourth quarter, we've got the ball on our own
two-yard line. Johnny gets the ball, cuts outside, and takes off

down the sideline with a guy chasing him, just a yard or two behind him. John scores, even though he just couldn't pull away from the guy.

John comes over to the sideline, panting, and I tell him, "Johnny, you're dogging it on me out there, and we've got Army in two weeks. That guy almost caught you." Out of breath, he said, "Coach, Coach, I ran as fast as I could. I couldn't go any faster." I said, "Okay, John." It turns out that the guy chasing him ran a 9.7. I guess all that extra work with Roger had paid off—apparently Johnny had gained an extra step or two of speed.

SKIP ORR:

Our Notre Dame trip was the most memorable away game that year. I think every Catholic kid in America followed Notre Dame, and growing up in the fifties Notre Dame was one of the few teams for which you could watch their highlights every week. I used to watch them all the time.

It was a cold, cloudy day, and this was a Notre Dame team in transition. They didn't have a typical great team, and Jack Snow and John Huarte were on the bench a lot, as juniors. It was a big thrill. We didn't play well in the first half, and I think it was 7-7 at halftime. Hardin came into the locker room and really chewed our butts. He talked about our having come too far to not win this game solidly. He also said something to the effect that we could lose Roger's chance to win the Heisman Trophy if we didn't play our best.

In the second half we went on to destroy them. Pat Donnelly had a great game, running for three touchdowns. It was in that game that I really got caught up in what we were accomplishing more than in any other game, outside of playing Army at the end of the season.

ROGER STAUBACH:

Then there was the Army game at the end of the season, following the assassination of President Kennedy. I can remember scoring two touchdowns in the second half to take a 21-7 lead and never getting the ball back again. They had a long drive and scored, and then recovered an onside kick and drove all the way down to inside our five-yard line before the game ended. They kept the ball more than a quarter on those last two drives.

I remember standing on the sideline with Coach Hardin and how he kept telling me what we were going to do once we got the ball back, which we never did. Their quarterback, Rollie Stichweh, was amazing—he just kept moving the ball on us. I said, "Hey, Coach, we're not going to get the ball back." Then they ran out of time-outs with the ball at our two-yard line. Suddenly, the game was over, and I can remember Tom Lynch grabbing the ball and running off the field.

That victory over Army really made our season. Losing to Texas in the Cotton Bowl put a damper on our season, but a loss to Army would have ruined it.

That whole season taught me a lot about teamwork. We had a great captain in Tom Lynch, who's now a retired admiral. I learned a lot about what it meant to pay the price together and to accomplish something, and we accomplished a lot together that year. The Heisman put me on the map as far as recognition goes, but it all related to our having a successful season as a team.

The 1963 Army-Navy game had been pushed back a week after the JFK assassination, which hit the team hard. Kennedy, a former navy man himself (watch PT 109 with Cliff Robertson in the Kennedy role), had been open about his support of the Midshipmen. WAYNE HARDIN *remembers:*

President Kennedy was very close to the Naval Academy and to the football team. It hit us like a ton of bricks. When we went to camp before the 1962 season, we trained at Quonset Point, a naval base in Rhode Island. We were practicing one time when we were told that the president was going to be landing at the airport and that Jackie was coming in from overseas, and they were going to meet there. I said, "Let's put a call in to his staff and see if he would like to come out and meet the team." Word came back to us that he would love to. *Air Force One* lands, and we had the team standing by, all in dress uniform, for inspection.

I introduced him to the players and gave him a football autographed by the team. He hadn't gone through ten guys when he said to his aide, "Go get Bobby (Kennedy). He's going to want to see this." So Bobby comes down, too. It was just a special occasion, and I just knew that he rooted for our team, although we also knew he had to be impartial at the Army-Navy game. I know one time after the game, I saw him as he was being driven away, and he looked at me and gave me the thumbs-up because we had won the game.

HARDIN continues by segueing into his account of the Army-Navy game that finally ensued:

It was difficult to play the game after the president's assassination. Paul Dietzel was the Army coach, and it was obvious from the start that his whole strategy was to keep Staubach off the field. If he could do that, then they would have a chance. So when they got the ball, they were taking their time getting into the huddle and taking their time breaking out of the huddle and coming to the line of scrimmage, snapping the ball one second before the play clock ran out. They were going to milk the clock all they could.

They kept the clock running as much as they could. They would run the ball and then take their time getting up. They'd lay on the pile, and then they wouldn't get up, they wouldn't get up, they wouldn't get up. They were wasting a lot of time. I never thought too much about it, and then we get to the end of the game and they have the ball. We're up, 21-15, and they have the ball around our fifty after recovering an onside kickoff.

There was about five or six minutes left in the game, certainly plenty of time to drive the ball down and score. As it turned out, they never scored and we never got the ball back. Then the game ended. They were still taking all the time they could between plays, staying on the ground in piles, and now it was working against them as time ran out. They couldn't change the pace, or at least they didn't try.

Roger and I were over on the sideline watching this. I turned to Roger and said, "You know if they score, we're going to have to have a two-minute offense ready to go," and we started talking about what we would have to do. Then it got down close to one minute, and they still had the ball driving toward our goal line. I said, "Rog, now we need to be thinking about a one-minute drill." And we had one. He said, "Okay, I got that." Then it got down to about thirty seconds, and I said, "Roger, I think now it's time to pray a little."

They got ready to snap the ball, the gun went off, and the official grabbed the ball and said, "This game is over." The ball was on the one-yard line. That was it—the game was over. Army had done everything they needed to, except they had run out of time. This is what happens when you program a team so tightly to run the clock, especially when you're talking about guys at a military school who are trained to follow orders. They did exactly what they had been ordered to do.

RICK FORZANO, *Navy assistant coach:*

Army just kept letting the clock run. On the last play, they came out of the huddle, had a mix-up in signals, and went back into the huddle. You can see it on film: You can see the head linesman moving in slowly. It gets down to one second and he puts his foot on the ball, and the center can't get the ball up. We win the game. I'm telling you, it was a riot. I don't know how many people saw that, but I was up in the press box watching this thing.

Navy hung on to defeat Army, only to go down to Texas the next month to get pounded the next month by Texas, 28-6, in the Navy-unfriendly confines of the Cotton Bowl, again, again. Was Texas that much better than Staubach's Middies?

STEVE BELICHECK:

There's a story behind that Cotton Bowl game with Texas, and it concerns Paul Dietzel, who was the head coach at Army at the time. Dietzel never impressed me. One time I was at an Army game preparing a scouting report, and I was talking to three writers from papers in the Baltimore-Washington area. We were just sitting around shooting the breeze and the subject of Dietzel came up. I said to them, "Dietzel doesn't really impress me. He's a phony. And that's off the record."

I went on to tell these guys how at every coaches' convention, when there are talks or seminars being given, that Dietzel, regardless of who's talking, would walk down and sit on the first row, carrying this big briefcase. One day he got up and left and forgot his briefcase, so someone grabbed it and opened it up. Empty. Not a thing in it.

The next morning, after I told this to these three writers, I open up a paper and see on the front page of the sports section where it says, "Navy Scout Likens Dietzel to Empty Briefcase." They ran the whole story. I really felt bad about it and was sort of ticked.

I don't see Dietzel again until the following year. I go to Pittsburgh with John Hopkins, another coaching assistant, to scout Army-Pittsburgh and to exchange films with them. When we get to the film room at Pittsburgh, someone comes up to tell

U.S. NAVAL ACADEMY

Staubach on graduation day at the Naval Academy, getting his boards put on by parents Robert and Betty Staubach as part of his commissioning ceremony.

us that the Army football team has just landed at the airport. We also needed to exchange film with the Army coaches, so I told John we might as well exchange with them now instead of waiting until the game tomorrow.

So we go to the airport to meet the team coming in. We're standing off to the side, and when Dietzel gets off the plane he sees me and walks over to me. He puts his arm around me and says, "Steve, my boy, I'm really sorry to see how you feel about me after all that we've been through together." And I said, "Wait, hold the phone. What in the hell have you and I been through together? We haven't been through anything together. You've been a head coach and I've been an assistant, and we've never been on the same staff. So we really don't have anything in common. I'm sorry that that thing came out in the paper the way that it did, but don't tell me about how we've been through everything together."

It was about twelve or fourteen years later, while I was attending a coaches' convention in Dallas, that I was walking along when a friend saw me and yelled at me. I walked over to talk with him, and there was this guy standing next to him—turns out to be a guy from the University of Texas—who looks and sees me and my badge that says "Naval Academy." This guy asks me, "Were you at Navy when we played you in the Cotton Bowl?"

"Yeah."

"You know what our favorite song was that year at Texas?."

"Uh, I would assume "The Eyes of Texas.'"

And he said, "Oh, no. It was 'On, Brave Old Army Team.'"

I said, "What the hell are you talking about?"

"Do you know that we had all your defensive signals? We knew what defense you were going to use the whole game."

Dietzel had given them all our signals. It's easy enough to chart someone's signals by having someone sit in the stands and then chart the signals against what plays were called, checking it against the game film. What Darrell Royal (the Texas head coach) would do was that as soon as he saw the defensive signal from our sideline, he would tell his quarterback what was coming, and then they could call a play to go away from what they knew we were going to do. I'm surprised more people don't do it.

To this day I'm sure that was a carryover from me and what I had said that got printed in the paper.

BELICHECK, *back on the subject of Staubach, the irrepress-ible competitor who never met a challenge he couldn't accept:*

I never saw anybody who competed like he did. During the summers, we used to have a football camp for high school kids. One summer not long after he graduated from the Naval Academy, Roger came up there to check out what was going on. One of the drills we had at the camp was a figure-eight run for the backs and wide receivers. Two identical courses were set up next to each other so we could run two kids off at a time to race against each other, with tackling dummies set up for the players to run around.

There was this one high school kid who was really quick, and Roger wanted to race him. So off they went. This kid kept beating Roger; not by much, a step or two, but Roger just wouldn't let him quit. He kept saying, "Let's go again. Let's go again." He was determined. Roger came back the next day and wanted to race the kid. Poor kid: To him it was just another race, but it meant a lot more to Roger. He couldn't stand losing to this kid.

It was the same after he got into the Navy and got sent to Vietnam as a supply officer. During his free time, he was always looking for someone he could throw a football around with, and sometimes that meant hopping into a jeep and driving forty or fifty miles when he heard there was a wide receiver in the area.

Staubach's football exploits were so noteworthy, that even higher brass with no real love for football were dropping anchor at Navy's games. BELICHECK:

I remember Bo Coppedge telling me about how some big admiral from Washington came to one of our games even though he didn't really love football or even know that much about it. But by the end of the third quarter of whatever game it was he was watching, this admiral was saying something like, "You know, Roger has been responsible for 267 yards," having figured all this in his head during the game. There were a lot of high-ranking naval officers, admirals included, who wanted Roger's autograph—and that was even before he got to the National Football League.

TOM LYNCH:

Being Roger's center on offense meant at least three things for me on every play: One, snap him the ball properly so he can do his thing; two, make sure I get a good block on the line of scrimmage so that nobody gets to him; and, three, be prepared to do another block and then another block because he's all over the place. And then, after he became renowned, some of the teams we played were singling him out and playing dirty ball with things like late hits, so the fourth thing became following him downfield to make sure guys coming in late wouldn't hit Roger. All of that made us a better team because he was a guy we really liked and respected—it wasn't all just Roger, Roger, Roger.

Almost forty years after the Cotton Bowl loss to Texas, ROGER STAUBACH, *now a Texas resident, has a hard time forgetting it:*

We really didn't have it together going into the Cotton Bowl. We had the big delay, almost a month, between games, and some of the guys were a little concerned about not having enough Christmas leave because we didn't get home a whole lot as it was.

We actually threw the ball very well against Texas, but their defense played a fantastic game keeping us bottled up.

I went into the Cotton Bowl Hall of Fame a few years ago, and I said to one of their guys, "Hey, we lost that game. Why am I going into the Hall of Fame?" And he said, "Well, you had a great game statistically, throwing for over two hundred yards in setting a Cotton Bowl game record, and you actually played very well." I said, "That doesn't matter because our job was to win the game. We lost the game." And he said, "Well, we have other losers in the Hall of Fame, too."

It was a really nice ceremony. Hugh Carlyle, the Texas quarterback from that game, went in the same time I did. When he got up there to make his acceptance speech, he said, "I'm just glad that Roger went into the Cotton Bowl Hall of Fame, because I knew if he was going in there I had to be going in, too. We beat them." All of these other Texas guys were there, like Darrell Royal, and there I was thinking, *Man, here I am trying to celebrate one of the worst losses of my career.* That was one of the two toughest losses of my career, the other one being the 35-31 loss to the Pittsburgh Steelers in the Super Bowl (after the 1978 season) when we were both vying to be the first team to win three Super Bowls.

Staubach was the most-scrutinized college football player in 1963. He was the most sought after by the media. But then, he might have been the least accessible of the Heisman Trophy candidates that year. With public relations director Budd Thalman *playing traffic cop, Staubach went about his Midshipman and academic duties six days a week without interruption. Thalman:*

Wayne Hardin didn't want Roger bothered with a whole lot of interviews. So we wouldn't let anybody talk to him during the week. The only time he was really available was after games. So there we were promoting him as a Heisman candidate while not letting anybody talk to him. that's something we would not have been able to get away with in 2002.

The demands on a Midshipman are pretty unique. You've got the military demands, the academic demands, and the athletic demands—and the military demands you really can't understate. You're up at five or six o'clock in the morning, and you have to report to formation, and they march to breakfast, lunch, and dinner. They have responsibilities in their various companies such as inspections. In a Midshipman's day, there wasn't a heckuva lot of time for interviews.

We took a little heat over that. Looking back, it probably wasn't the best thing to do, but it worked.

Roger was never a great interview. He was certainly willing and cooperative, but he wasn't the kind of guy who offered up a whole lot. He wasn't a colorful quote machine. He was always very modest and looking to share credit, and he always felt some form of empathy for the other team.

The more interviews you do over time, the better you get. But when you're twenty years old, it's all very new to you. In 1963 he had a roommate named Dick Smith, so I set up all kinds of interviews with Dick Smith. After a while, Dick Smith had become one of the most famous guys at the Naval Academy. He was a great interview.

THALMAN:

One of the things that happened in 1963 and which was unique in the world of athletics, is that Roger was on the cover of *Time*, which was very rare in sports, because in those days all the covers of *Time* were painted portraits. That was in October 1963. He also appeared on the covers of *Life* and *Sports Illustrated*, giving him the *Time* magazine trifecta. At least, sort of.

I remember when the guy from *Life* magazine called me about Roger's being on the cover, and I asked the guy if there was anything that could keep Roger off. He said, "Only some sort of catastrophe." Well, there was a catastrophe—Kennedy was assassinated. The *Life* cover that Roger appeared on never got distributed. They ran a million copies and threw all of them away but three. Roger has one of them, I have one, and the superintendent of the Naval Academy at the time had one.

When the official word came down that Staubach had won the Heisman, it was time for THALMAN *and his star to head for the bright lights of New York City:*

In those days, when you won the Heisman Trophy, they notified you by telegram. Roger was very modest about it and said that everyone should have shared in it. We still had to play the Army-Navy game, which had been delayed a week because of the Kennedy assassination.

We go to New York, and Roger goes with Marianne and his parents. I'm going to haul them all to the Ed Sullivan Theater, where he's going to be on the *Ed Sullivan Show*. Roger goes on the show and goes out on stage dressed in his navy uniform. Ed is asking him several questions, when all of a sudden Roger put his hand under his chin and waves his fingers like some kind of dope.

After the show I asked him, "What were you doing?! What were you thinking?!" And he said, "I told the guys back at the Yard that I would wave to them."

THALMAN *continues:*

Tom Lynch was in New York, too, because he was the captain of the team. The superintendent and athletic director decided to take Lynch to the Heisman Trophy dinner as well.

A night or two before the dinner, Roger and Tom come to me and tell me that they want to go to the Playboy Club, which was in Times Square. I offered to call ahead to tell the club that these two guys would be coming, but they said no, that they didn't want to make a big deal out of it.

The problem was, Roger only had his navy uniform. He didn't have any civilian clothes with him. He said, "I don't want to go to the Playboy Club in my uniform." So I took off my trousers and jacket, which was straining to fit Roger, and gave them to Roger to wear. He kept his own shirt and black tie on.

So he and Lynch head out to the Playboy Club, and only about a half-hour later they're back. I asked, "What happened?" They said they couldn't get in. I asked them, "Did you tell them who you were?"

"No, we didn't tell them who we were."

"So, what did you do?"

"We went to a restaurant in Times Square, got a milk shake, and came back."

"Tell you what—you guys are two dandies." I mean, these two guys went to see the Playboy Club and came back with two milk shakes instead. Talk about opposite ends of the spectrum.

I also remember taking Roger to a photo studio to have a photo layout made for *Sports Illustrated*, which was to recognize the top sports personalities of 1963. We get to the studio, and the guy doing the photo shoot is obviously gay. Roger is uncomfortable as hell, as am I, and this guy had Roger doing these unusual poses, such as one arm behind the back. Roger is saying to me, "What is this guy doing?"

JOE BELLINO *had won the Heisman three years earlier, and he could feel himself in Staubach's spit-shined shoes:*

It was altogether different back then. There was some publicizing and promotion, but not much. Still, the actual announcement had as much glamour then as it does now, even though it wasn't nationally televised. The attention you got in New York City doing TV and radio there was as big then as it is now.

During the season, the Heisman Trophy was the furthest thing from my mind. I was more concerned with school, my grades, carrying out my Midshipman duties, and winning football games.

I can remember the last game of the year, against Army. We were heavily favored and went into the second half ahead, 17-0, and it was looking like a blowout. Lo and behold, Army comes back and gets to within 17-12. We get the ball back on our own thirty with about five minutes to go. I take the handoff, get hit, and fumble the ball away in the backfield. Now it looks like we're going to lose.

Fortunately, back then we played both ways, and so I got to stay on the field on defense. I was in on every play, doing everything I could to make sure that fumble would not be too costly. I caused a fumble that we weren't able to recover, but on the last play of the series, I intercepted a pass in the end zone and brought the ball out to the fifty-yard line, and that's how the game ended.

After the game, the publicity director at the Naval Academy, John Cox, comes up to me, gives me a big hug, and says, "Hey, Joey, that last play made you win the Heisman Trophy." I said, "Win the Heisman Trophy? That last play saved me from being the goat of the game." That's what I was thinking.

BELLINO *offers this further perspective on the Heisman and what it entails:*

All of us who are Heisman Trophy winners realize that when we were winning the award, there was at least one other player out there somewhere who was bigger, better, faster, and a better player, but for whatever reason he got hurt or wasn't on the right team. We all know that we were at the right place at the right time and did the right things.

My last year, everything clicked. We played the right teams and upset the right teams, and we got ourselves onto national television even though we had been unranked at the beginning of the season. We played in the Northeast; we played in the Southeast; we played in the Northwest; we played in the Southwest—we played in every section of the country, and that kind of exposure helped me win the trophy.

Every year all of us past winners who are still alive go to the award ceremony, and we just go there with a big smile and we sit in front one tier down from the present winner. We all have to turn back in our chairs to see the winner, and when we do it we all know that the kid does not know what he's won and he won't know it until twenty or twenty-five years down the road. You have to live it to fully experience what it means. Many of us get streets and gymnasiums named after us, and these guys don't even know that stuff like that is going to be coming.

WAYNE HARDIN *coached Navy from 1959 to 1964 and compiled a 38-22-2 record there. He also coached two Heisman Trophy winners in a four-year stretch, Joe Bellino, the 1960 winner, and Roger Staubach, 1963. Hardin compares and contrasts the two:*

Both players were fortunate to have a lot of good talent around them, as both teams went 9-1 (during the regular season) and played in a major bowl game.

I did the same thing with both teams when it came to team meetings, and that was to try and get all the players to understand that each guy, Joe and Roger, would get a lot of headlines, but they would be unable to be successful without a good team around them. Basically, I told them when they read the headlines to put their own names in place in there because they deserved it.

As similar as Joe and Roger were in terms of being great players and great guys with a terrific work ethic, they came out of different situations. Joe is a story in himself. He came from an old Italian family with a philosophy of where once you completed high school, you went out and got a job to help pay your dad back for all that he had done for you over the years. Joe was able to come to Annapolis because his siblings said they would work to pay his share that went back into the family.

Joe, like Roger, is a super human being and a credit to society. He was the best football player I've ever seen one-on-one, and I know I could get an argument out of that. But I can't remember too many times where just one guy could bring Joe down.

With Joe and Roger you had two great athletes. So, what made them different; what sets them apart from others with similar athletic ability? I say that most people have five senses, if they're lucky, and both Joe and Roger had a sixth sense. I mean, really . . . a sixth sense. I know you hear that bandied about with some people, but I don't know how else to say it, except that it was something truly genuine with those two guys. It's like built-in radar.

STEVE BELICHECK:

Bellino and Roger were both top-notch guys; both were devout Catholics. I told Joe that of all the running backs I ever saw in college, I thought he was the best. After his second step, he was running full speed. And he had great vision; he could see the whole field around him. Some of the runs he made were unbelievable. He did have one problem, and that is he was so muscular that he used to get cramps a lot. He could play defense, too, and was a helluva punt and kickoff returner. Who was the better athlete between the two? I wouldn't want to make that call. They were both unbelievable athletes.

So whatever happened to Staubach's Heisman hardware?
BUDD THALMAN *offers a few answers:*

I was the public relations director for the Buffalo Bills when they played at Dallas in a game sometime after he had retired, and I went to his house and spent some time with him. That's when I saw the setup with the basketball court, his place for working out with weights, and how he had his Heisman trophy on a lower mantel that was sort of out of the way, not easy to spot.

One of my favorite Roger stories took place soon after he won the Heisman Trophy in December 1963. He had to come back to campus after the ceremony because it wasn't yet time to go home for Christmas vacation. He didn't want to keep the trophy in his dorm room during that time because he felt like that would be showing off. So he gave it to me to take care of it.

I didn't know where to put it, so I put it in the trunk of my car. I went to the grocery store one day, and when the kid came out to the car carrying my groceries, I popped open the trunk and told him, "Put the groceries right in there, next to the Heisman Trophy." The kid was dumbstruck.

Serving in the navy or any branch of the military can involve
life-and-death scenarios wrapped around lots of laughs, fun,
and games. PAT DONNELLY *lived through one such story that*

took place while he, Staubach, and Skip Orr were away in Europe, even though the international tensions weren't of the usual wartime variety. You will notice that when the going got really tough, as happenstance would have it, Staubach was not out in front—his teammates were. Donnelly recalls:

We were on our first-class cruise in the Mediterranean between our junior and senior years. Roger and I were on a guided-missile frigate, and Skip Orr was on another ship in the same battle group. We had decided before we went that instead of coming back to the U.S. after the cruise ended, we were going to spend two or three weeks in Europe sightseeing.

We were anchored off Cannes, France. We stayed there for a few days, and while there we rented two motorcycles, more like motor scooters, with two of us being able to ride together on the bigger of the two bikes.

One of the excursions we took was to Monte Carlo. Skip and I doubled up on one and Roger was on the other. When we got to Monte Carlo, we went to the casino there and were having a really good time. You had to wear a coat and tie to get into the casino, so we were dressed up. We ended up playing craps. Now that I think about it, we could have been living out our own James Bond movie, although the girls came later during the cruise.

Back to the craps table. I remember there was a seedy guy nearby. At one point, Skip threw his dice and won, and as he was reaching to pick up his chips, this other guy reached in and snatched them. Skip grabbed the guy's hand and said, "Hey, those are my winnings." The guy started yelling at Skip in French, and then started making a big scene when security surrounded him. I think the security guys knew what was going on, but they let the other guy keep the winnings, gave Skip an equal amount, and then they kicked this other guy out.

It was about one in the morning when we decided it was time to head back to our hotel room in Cannes, and we were kind of giddy. We hadn't been drinking—we were at least smart enough to not do that while riding motorcycles. It was about twenty-five to thirty miles back, all along a beautiful highway on top of a cliff overlooking the Mediterranean.

The highway was winding, and we came to a curve where there was a cliff up the hill on the right side and a cliff down to the sea on the left side. It was kind of a blind curve and a little sharper than I had anticipated. Coming in the other direction was a car coming too fast, and he was cutting across the center line. Skip and I were riding in front on our bike, and Roger was a little way behind us on his.

That's when things sort of flashed before my eyes, and it seemed there was no way we could avoid a head-on collision. As I recall, as I turned toward the right, we were basically skidding right toward the front of the car. We ended up sideswiping him, at which time I lost control of the motorcycle. Skip by then had pushed himself off the back of the bike, and he's skidding along the road and I'm still on the motorcycle, which crashed into the guardrail on the downslope side, and I was skidding along the pavement as well.

Skip and I had our helmets on, but I'm lying on the pavement trying to figure if I was dead or had broken bones. I was numb and bleeding a lot. No serious injury, but a lot of scrapes all over the body from the gravel on the road. Same for Skip. Roger was behind us, watching all this happen, as he pulled off to the side of the road. He was thinking major catastrophe.

Skip could speak French and he started talking to the driver, and then we figured we needed to get some medical attention. As beaten up as it was, the motorcycle still ran. We found a police station that was closed, and then exchanged information with the driver. We parted company and went back to a pharmacy, where this guy swabbed us with hydrogen peroxide and plucked out the gravel imbedded in our skin. It could have been an unhappy ending but for the grace of God.

Now for the rest of the Ian Fleming saga. DONNELLY:

On that first-class cruise, we were anchored off Athens, Greece, at one point. The commander of the battle group invited some of us midshipmen to a picnic on one of the offshore islands using his captain's gig, which was a large cabin cruiser, like a yacht.

The condition was we had to bring a date, and not many of us knew anyone in Athens. We decided the best way to do this was to go to a beach outside of Athens, find some prospects, and invite them. Roger met a Canadian girl and invited her, and she agreed to come. She didn't have any friends with her, so out of the blue I approached a nice-looking Greek girl. I couldn't speak much Greek and she couldn't speak much English, but we communicated well and she understood what I was asking and agreed to come to the picnic.

We all had a good time, and Roger clearly was enjoying the company of the Canadian girl. He asked her out again, but she was busy or unavailable for whatever reason, and it didn't happen. He made his joking comment about her being heartbroken somewhere in Athens, but we had to leave there before he could see her again.

All this time Roger was still good friends with Marianne and they were still seeing each other when they had the opportunity. But they had agreed sometime before that it would be okay for each of them to date other people. The one that Roger seemed most concerned about was a girl who lived in Washington, D.C., that he met late in his senior year. He went out with her several weekends in a row, and he became concerned—he was going to have to make a decision. He finally decided that Marianne was too important to him, so he handed this other girl from D.C. off to me as well.

Back in America and at Annapolis, there still was a 1964 season to be played, even though Staubach had already been drafted by the NFL's Cowboys and the Kansas City Chiefs of the upstart American Football League (Staubach was eligible for the 1964 draft as a junior because his high school class was now graduating college and he had spent that first year in

New Mexico). SKIP ORR *takes us into the 1964 season, which*
turned out to be a post-1963 bummer:

Navy continued to play two-way when it didn't have to for a while
longer. You had a defensive specialist who could substitute for the
quarterback. Everybody else played two ways. I don't think it was
ever a consideration for Roger to play both ways, although he
could have. He was tough enough to do it.

First game our senior season, in 1964, we went up and beat
Penn State, 21-8. But Roger got hurt in that game (severely
sprained ankle), and never really got back to 100 percent that season. He ended up wearing a high-top shoe and something like a
hockey puck on his heel so it wouldn't aggravate the injury more.
In the limited time he could play, he had to throw a lot; he
couldn't scramble, so that took away a lot of his effectiveness.

He threw the ball a lot that year, but we just never jelled. Plus
there were other injuries: Pat Donnelly got hurt against
California, I injured a knee against Pitt. We were both hobbled
pretty much the rest of the year, and we ended up playing more
defense than we did offense. Penn State went on to win the
Lambert Trophy as the best team in the East, and we ended up
going 3-6-1. It was a disaster.

We still had some really good talent on that 1964 team, but
we didn't have the kind of depth that can compensate for a few
injuries. You look now and see ninety guys dressed up for a game,
and we had forty-four guys, that was it. We never saw the need to
have more: We thought, *How could you possibly play more than*
forty-four people in a game? And a lot of those guys wouldn't even
get into the game. Basically, you had three teams of guys who saw
playing time and a fourth team that supplanted those first three.
It was totally different. I went to the Navy spring game this year,
and when they introduced the coaches—just the coaches—I
counted sixteen. How many coaches did we have? We had about
six. What do they all do?

BUDD THALMAN, *on the 1964 letdown:*

There was a lot of talk about winning a second Heisman; Roger obviously was the leader in the clubhouse going into the season. As a matter of fact, let me read the quote he signed to me in his book *First Down: A Lifetime to Go.* "To Budd Thalman: Best wishes to the guy who held me back from a second Heisman Trophy." He's always had this very wry sense of humor. He's a really funny guy, but you wouldn't know it unless you were around him enough to understand it.

For Navy or either of the other service academies to compete for a national title, it would take a freak of nature. But back in the early sixties, it was still reasonable for either Army or Navy to be nationally ranked sometime during the season. Remember, too, that in the nineteen seasons between 1945 and 1963 inclusive, Army and Navy produced five Heisman Trophy winners between them (Army's Doc Blanchard in 1945, Glenn Davis in 1946, and Pete Dawkins in 1958, and Navy's Bellino in 1960 and Staubach in 1963). Navy's number-two finish marked the last time either Army or Navy seriously contended for a national championship, and that's basically forty years ago. Nineteen sixty-three also marked the last time (going into 2002, at least) that Navy beat Notre Dame, and they've played every season since. SKIP ORR *offers his take, from Navy's perspective, on life after Staubach, Lynch, Donnelly, Orr et al:*

In the early sixties it was starting to be an aberration that the service academies could compete well on a national level, but it still wasn't unusual for a Navy team to beat someone like Notre Dame or go out to the West Coast and beat Washington. Just look at the schedule we were playing in 1963 and 1964: Michigan and Pittsburgh always had strong teams; Penn State, Notre Dame, Georgia Tech—teams that were strong.

Look at the West Virginia team that we beat, 51-7, to open the 1963 team. That team had been specially recruited because it was the centennial year for the state of West Virginia—they had emblems on their helmets and their jerseys and they had increased the size of their stadium, so they were really gearing for that season. And they weren't that bad a football team. We just went out there and put it all together. We couldn't do anything wrong that day, and it was in their stadium.

We didn't think things would change with the service academies as much and as rapidly as they did. In the George Welsh era, Navy had some competitive teams that went to bowl games, but I don't think their ranking ever got up into the top fifteen or so.

Maybe you can point at the mid-sixties as the start of the downfall for the service academies. By that time you had the NFL and the AFL competing for talent. Prior to that, in the late fifties, and early sixties, pro football was seen as a nice job, but only the key players were making a lot of money. But then came the NFL and AFL bidding war that jacked up salaries and began the days of the big bonuses. For a high school kid who's a quality blue-chip player, what's he thinking now? *I can play pro football and make a lot of money.* Plus the leagues had expanded, providing more opportunities to do it. So now you're a Naval Academy recruiter going to talk to a kid who's being told by all these other schools that "if you go to the Naval Academy, it's highly unlikely that you'll ever play pro football."

Although ROGER STAUBACH *had been drafted in 1964, everyone knew it would be at least four years before he would get his shot at pro football. Staubach did get a chance to leave one last impression on the heels of the disappointing 1964 season:*

The thing that kept me credible was the College All-Star game after my senior year. We were up against the Cleveland Browns, and although we finally lost, 24-16, I had a pretty good first quarter. Then an injury to my left shoulder put me out. It was a dislocation. I remember that Paul Warfield was also hurt, and he was getting a cracked collarbone treated in the training room, so I had to take my first aid in the locker room. The doctor braced his arm in my armpit and cranked my arm, but it

U.S. NAVAL ACADEMY, ELSBURGH CLARKE

Staubach frequently returns to his alma mater, where he is duly recognized as a true Midshipman legend.

was no go. Later I had to have surgery. Still, the pro scouts must have liked what little they'd seen of me under pressure from real football players, because both Kansas City and Dallas wanted to sign me.[1]

BILL BUSIK:

When you talk about Roger, you've got to remember that he also played other sports. I'll never forget one baseball game in which he laid down a bunt and again separated his shoulder sliding into first base. They took him up to the hospital, got his shoulder put back in place, and he came back and pitched the rest of the game.

On top of that he was so religious. Every morning he was over at the chapel. Everything about him was so solid. The intensity with which he played on the field was so diametrically opposite to what you saw in him when you sat down to talk to him. You put that uniform on him, and he became a holy terror. This guy was vicious out there.

BUSIK *continues:*

After being athletic director, I became a special assistant for liaison and public affairs to the chief of naval personnel. I thought Roger, who by this time was a supply officer over in Vietnam, needed to be recruiting for the navy. I did a little study of supply officers and found that we had plenty of them, more than enough to fill all the slots. So I ran a piece of paper around the circuit changing the rules on supply officers, and I got it signed off because everyone along the way knew I had a vested interest in this. Roger got assigned to Pensacola and played football down there. That's how he stayed in shape, and, of course, he already had his Dallas Cowboys' contract in his hip pocket. He would have kept in shape pretty much anyway.

At the same time, a lot of the supply corps officers had been lopped off because the navy had too many of them. A lot of people misunderstood that and said that we did it (only) for Roger. We did it for a lot of other guys, too, because we had to. I was just making sure that the navy's best interests were being served, and Roger's being available in the public eye to embody the image of the naval officer was serving the navy's best interests. All he had to do in Dallas was play football, get on TV, and talk about the Naval Academy when he had the chance.

TEX SCHRAMM, *longtime Cowboys general manager, recalls drafting Staubach:*

I was in the room at the time of the pick, and I remember thinking that any time you have a chance to get a great football player, you do it. This wasn't much of a gamble except from the standpoint of time. All it cost was a tenth-round pick. He still had another year at the Naval Academy, and it was very clear from the outset that he also was going to fulfill his four-year obligation to the navy.

Roger had already been drafted by the Kansas City Chiefs, and all of a sudden they were trying to sign him. We went up to Philadelphia for a game, and Roger was also up there for the Army-Navy game, and we were able to get together. We made the deal with him and offered to pay him a certain amount of money while he was in the navy ($500 a month, plus a $10,000 signing bonus).

JOE BELLINO, who graduated from Annapolis in 1961, had been there done that, having played three years in the NFL with the Boston Patriots following his four-year stint in the navy:

By the third year with the Patriots, I was playing as well as I ever had, and all my football instincts had come back to me. The hard part was the mental part of the game. I had lost my instincts, such as what to do when carrying the ball into a hole or trying to catch a punt. I could still do those things, but had to think about them a little. It took a couple of years to come back.

Roger played a lot of football during his four years in the navy, and I didn't. He also went to training camp with the Cowboys while in the navy, so in that respect he wasn't fully out of the game. I never saw him play while he was at Navy, so I didn't have anything to go on when assessing how he played when he went to the Cowboys (in 1969). When Roger was winning his Heisman in 1963, I was bouncing around on a minesweeper in the South China Sea. From what I can tell, he had some difficulty his first year or two, but then he came into his own.

FROM NEXT YEAR'S CHAMPIONS TO AMERICA'S TEAM

*F*OR ALMOST TEN YEARS before Roger Staubach made it to the National Football League, and for more than ten years after he retired, the Dallas Cowboys failed to win a Super Bowl or a league/conference championship. But for the eleven seasons that Staubach was a part of the club, the Cowboys went to five Super Bowls, winning two (24-3 over Miami in Super Bowl VI in 1972, and 27-10 over Denver in Super Bowl XII in 1978), and played in seven NFC Championship games, winning five.

By the time that Staubach had retired in March 1980, the Cowboys were firmly entrenched as "America's Team," at least in the sense that they laid claim to that title before anyone else—e.g., the Pittsburgh Steelers—had thought to do so. Before Staubach came to the Cowboys in 1969 as a twenty-seven-year-old rookie, the best the franchise could do was "Next Year's Champions," a moniker that sounds complimentary, or at least optimistic, until it sinks in.

Between the team's expansion birth in 1960 and 1968, the Cowboys had matured from an 0-11-1 start and a total of five losing seasons to being a seasoned playoff participant that twice played the Green Bay Packers (after the 1966 and 1967 seasons) for the right to go to the Super Bowl and then twice lost to the Cleveland Browns (1968 and 1969) in Eastern Conference championship games after posting the league's best record both seasons. Alas, next year's champions.

By this time, Staubach was on board as the heir nonapparent to popular quarterback Don Meredith, who had suddenly retired at age thirty-one in July 1969. Third-string quarterback Jerry Rhome had been traded away a few months earlier. And with those two moves, Staubach had jumped from number-four quarterback to number two on the Cowboys' depth chart, leaving him and number-one Craig Morton to battle back and forth over the next five-plus years. Once Staubach had the reins all to himself, then it was okay to break out the "Hail Marys" and celebrate "America's Team."

LEE ROY JORDAN, *who would eventually become Staubach's road and training-camp roomie, came to the Cowboys out of Alabama in 1963, finding a young football team on a mission:*

Coach (Tom) Landry had a vision of what he was going to do and had a good core foundation started. At least he was able to convince me that an expansion team wasn't a bad thing to be with. That's why I came to Dallas rather than going to play for the Boston Patriots in the AFL, which had drafted me with their first pick.

Nineteen sixty-five was a big year for us. We ended up 7-7 and beat some good opponents, such as the Giants and the Steelers. And we ended up going to what they called "the Loser Bowl" back then, the two division runner-ups. We played the Colts in a little playoff game down in Miami. We didn't play too good, but we sure had a good time in going. That was the turning point for the

Cowboys in making us realize that we had a lot of talent, and that with experience we could be a good football team. It took us a long time, but we finally did prove that after struggling through some great seasons in which we were unable to win it all, like when we lost to the Green Bay Packers in the playoffs in two consecutive years.

Back then the compliments were not easy to take sometimes, such as when people referred to us as "Next Year's Champions." It sounds good when you first hear it, but then you come to not appreciate it after you've heard it repeated a few times. We were close, but we were young, where the Packers were quite mature and went on to win the first two Super Bowls. We came back and played well in '68 and '69, but blew it in the playoffs, both times against the Cleveland Browns. I think it was a combination perhaps of Coach Landry and a young coaching staff not preparing us as well as they could have and our being a team that didn't have the confidence we needed to have in those playoff games.

Don Meredith took most of the criticism for our losing those playoff games. It wasn't fair to Don. Coach Landry didn't deflect any of that criticism from Don, even though he could have. That's just the way Coach Landry was, although Don certainly didn't deserve the criticism for those losses. Consequently, he retired prematurely, I think.

I was shocked when he retired. I thought Don was a great quarterback who didn't have the greatest of offensive lines to work with. He got beat up a lot during those early years, and we were just getting the type of quality in the offensive line that you could depend on. We had finally gotten to the point that we could have some balance on offense, with both a running game and a passing game. Don felt like the criticism was singled out for him too much.

Tom didn't try to persuade people to do things, such as trying to talk Don out of retirement. Don was looking for someone to encourage and control him, to convince him to play longer, and he didn't get it. I also think Don was going through some changes in his personal life as well, and he was looking for someone to be there for him. It didn't work out that way.

In drafting Staubach in the tenth round of the 1964 NFL Draft,
the Cowboys were exercising a draft philosophy of sometimes
doing the unusual, which in Staubach's case was true because
he was still five years away from being about to play. Cowboys
director of player personnel GIL BRANDT *explains:*

Over the years we drafted guys like Roger, Herschel Walker, and
Bob Hayes because they were available somewhere in a middle
round of the draft, and the odds of your finding a really good football player that late in the draft anyway is pretty slim. It was worth
the risk of taking someone like that who had great payoff potential in the long run. If they didn't work out, then we really weren't
that worse off.

When we visited college campuses, we didn't restrict our vis-
its to the football offices—we also went to the basketball offices.
One of the great relationships we had was with Bob Knight. We
signed one of his guys, who, although he couldn't earn a spot
with us, ended up playing seven or eight years with the
(Cincinnati) Bengals.

Cornell Green had been a basketball player who never played
college football. It's creative only if you have a head coach who
understands that you are drafting an athlete that you have to make
into a player. We also had players from schools that hardly anyone
had ever heard of—Fort Valley State, which is where Rayfield
Wright came from; from Elizabeth City State, Jethro Pugh; from
Virginia Union, Herb Scott—all became Pro Bowl players.

One thing we did with all these guys was pay them a bonus
that would go toward the purchase of a house in the Dallas area,
and we were able to keep all those guys in Dallas. So instead of a
guy being back in the off-season to Virginia, Wisconsin, or wherever it may be, we had all those guys working out every day at the
practice field because they lived nearby. We also had a great
group of wives, and what we ended up with was a great chemistry
in that we had guys who away from the field would go hunting

together or fishing together or going to play golf together.

At the end of the preseason, we would have a get-together at Royal Oaks Country Club on a Friday and have a cookout at night with all of the players and their families. In the afternoon, we'd get all of our players to play golf and get all these business people from the Dallas area to play along with them. They established a good relationship between the business

DALLAS COWBOYS

Staubach in a familiar scene with the Cowboys, out of the pocket and on the move.

community and the players, and on top of that we had players with great character. Roger probably was at the top of the flow chart because everybody looked up to the guy as someone who had also served in the service and was a guy who never complained. A lot of our success was because of people like Roger.

Brandt and the Cowboys brass gained a reputation as computer geeks who could analyze thousands of bits of information to extrapolate the best players to draft and the best plays to run against a particular opponent. BRANDT:

We were able to do a lot of things with the Cowboys because we had the money and resources to do them. We were using a computer in 1962 before most people knew what a computer was, and now people would be lost without it. We did all the things we could to study talent.

I say that the Cowboys are like McDonald's because you never see a boarded-up McDonald's. The reason you never see a boarded-up McDonald's is that they have studied in great detail how many cars go past a certain area at a certain time. They have a very good idea of how many of those cars are going to stop for food at a McDonald's if it's there.

Everything we did in scouting and everything Tom did in coaching and preparation was all based on previous history. So, that location at Fourth and Main may change, but past history shows that that is a good place. Same thing with running plays. And with a computer, we were up to date every week with every possible tendency and what we were gaining with every kind of play. It's almost like being able to find a way to flip a coin and have it come up heads 55 percent of the time, which if you can do, you will win every time.

TOM LANDRY *weighs in on the drafting of Staubach:*

We drafted him as a future prospect. But we didn't think he would be much. He had to sit out four years, and in those days we didn't think anyone could lay out even one year and come back and play football.[1]

GIL BRANDT:

We knew he was something special; otherwise we wouldn't have drafted him. What you banked on was Roger's being a guy who loved sports and loved to play football. He was what you would call an educated gym rat. A lot of times when people are away from something for a while, they have a hard time returning. They don't have the study habits and they are no longer structured—that's usually the case. With Roger, his whole life was structured. He knew where he wanted to go and how he was going to get there.

Outgoing Dallas Cowboys starting quarterback DON MEREDITH, *whose good-ole-boy sense of humor became legend on* Monday Night Football *telecasts, once took a playful poke at the rookie Roger Staubach's choirboy image:*

Staubach is going to have to learn what an NFL quarterback is like. He's going to have to grow his hair long and start smoking and drinking to keep up the image.[2]

DAN REEVES, *who went on to become a longtime Cowboys assistant coach before moving on to coach in Denver and Atlanta, played running back behind Meredith for several years. Reeves had this to say about Meredith:*

Don Meredith had tremendous talent, but he played the game more for the fun of it than he did the seriousness of it. If he had been as dedicated as John (Elway), no telling what he would have accomplished.

He was very competitive once the game began, but he didn't want to pay the price to be that great. He was a very good quarterback who could have been one of the all-time great quarterbacks. And, of course, that always led to friction with Coach (Tom) Landry, who couldn't understand that kind of thinking.[3]

STAUBACH *never played alongside Meredith, but he gave his predecessor ample praise:*

Don Meredith would have taken Dallas to some Super Bowl victories in the 1970s. Don Meredith was a very good quarterback, and he had the confidence of the team. Some of the players may have questioned Don's discipline at times as far as his fun, but when it came time to play, Don played hurt and he played tough. I think if he would have stayed in Dallas, I would have left. 'Cause I was going to be a starter in the NFL. I would never, ever have allowed myself to be relegated to a backup role for my whole career. I couldn't have handled it. Don would have been very difficult to unseat. Because Landry would not have replaced Don Meredith.[4]

Adds TEX SCHRAMM, *former Cowboys general manager:*

Don Meredith quit when he was thirty-one years old, and some guys are just getting going when they are thirty-one. He came back to me a year after he quit and he told me that he could still play. I think he missed it terribly and wanted to come back, but he didn't because he didn't want to go back on something that he had said about quitting. If Don had stayed with the Cowboys, I would not have wanted to be the one who had to make the choice as to which quarterback, or quarterbacks, to keep. There was something about Don that I knew, had he continued to play, he would have become even more of a success. He was a leader, and he should have played out his career, at least another three or four years.

Running back WALT GARRISON *came out of college a year after Staubach did, but he already was a grizzled veteran with three years' experience by the time Staubach was a rookie:*

He was the oldest rookie I had ever seen, and that made it hard to poke fun at him.

We got him into trouble one night. After the last game of two-a-days, the veterans got to stay out to midnight. We all went out and had a few beers and a good steak and so on. Roger went with us. Well, with him being a rookie, he was supposed to be back in by eleven o'clock. We told him not to worry about it, saying, "Gosh dang it, Roger, Tom Landry's not going to fine you. You're a twenty-seven-year-old rookie for Pete's sake."

He said okay and stayed out with us. Sure enough, when he got back to his room there was a note on his door telling him to see Coach Landry. Roger got fined pretty good for that. That was the last time he believed any of us.

GARRISON *continues:*

Roger Staubach . . . was a different kind of person than your normal Homo sapiens. He'd be out on a destroyer in the Gulf of Tonkin or some ungodly place for nine months at a time and then he'd take his leave and come to training camp and work out! . . . The guy had been off serving his country for eleven months, and he gets three weeks off and he's out there every day working his butt off. Training camp is exactly like going to boot camp all over again. In fact, I've been to both boot camp and training camp, and I'd rather go to boot camp. But Roger'd be out there with us every year.[5]

Running back CALVIN HILL *was drafted out of Yale in 1969 as the Cowboys' number-one pick and as the heir apparent to Dan Reeves and Craig Baynham at running back. Staubach and Hill were both rookies that year and they became good friends, although for Hill that meant having to overcome a mild case of hero worship:*

I was drafted in 1969. Roger and I were rookies together. Not only had Don Meredith retired, but so had Don Perkins, and Dan Reeves was about to retire. So almost all of the backfield was gone that year, the same backfield that had gone to NFC Championship games each of the previous two years. At that point, they were called Next Year's Champions.

It was an interesting time to come. I had been drafted out of Yale, and Roger had been to the two previous training camps. I'm from Baltimore originally, so I had always been a big Navy fan and was a Joe Bellino fan in the early sixties, followed by Roger a few years later. I was well aware of who guys like Tom Lynch, Skip Orr, and Pat Donnelly—some of Roger's teammates at Annapolis—were. I died with them when they lost to Texas in the 1964 Cotton Bowl. I went to a prep school up in New York called Riverdale Country School. Most of the people there were Army fans, given the proximity of West Point. During Army-Navy week, I was the one guy rooting for Navy.

The first day of training camp with the Cowboys, I was in the mess line, when I turn around and see Roger Staubach coming down the stairs into the cafeteria. He's right behind me and he says, "You must be Calvin Hill." I was delighted that he even knew who I was, his being the Heisman Trophy guy who had been away in Vietnam serving his country.

We had 105 rookies in that first week of camp, and they were dropping out very quickly. It was a remarkable story that Roger was coming back and trying to play after being out four years. He was the big story among the rookies, where in my case there was some question about whether or not the computer had made some kind of mistake, or been unplugged. In spite of his status coming in.

There used to be first-class citizenship and second-class citizenship, with veterans comprising the former and rookies the latter. Roger, by virtue of having competed against some of these vets in college and having been to the last two training camps, was given preferred status. But he chose to remain a rookie.

As Cowboys head coach, Tom Landry didn't believe in simplicity, not when it came to devising his defense and not when it came to planning his offense. The Landry System was complicated and required blind faith and loyalty from coaches and players. HILL:

It was especially difficult for a quarterback. You're not always sure what you're doing or why you're doing it. Roger was in an accelerated program because he wanted to play, and you've got to remember that Roger had actually been a contemporary of Craig's because they had competed against each other in college.

Roger was determined to do everything he could to accelerate that learning curve. He was twenty-seven and needed to hit the field running. Landry believed strongly that his system took time to learn, maybe four to five years to develop a quarterback. Craig had served his apprenticeship under Don Meredith. There were things that Craig understood and Roger didn't, and I think that frustrated Roger. Craig knew the plays and what everybody was doing, and Roger didn't all the time.

HILL *continues:*

I was confused early my rookie year because for the first two weeks they weren't sure where they were going to play me. They put me at linebacker, running back, and tight end. I was even more confused than Roger. I had been a quarterback in high school but played running back all through college. I had also been a linebacker while playing both ways back in high school.

They thought it would probably take me two years to make the transition from the Ivy League to the NFL, not having had the benefit of spring football at Yale. Actually, we did—it lasted one day, consisting essentially of a morning practice and a picnic in the afternoon. They figured that the football season itself was enough of a burden on your life as a student.

I left training camp for two weeks to take part in the College All-Star game, and when I came back Dan Reeves had still not come back from his surgery. His backup was a guy named Craig Baynham, and he had injured a rib. By now, we were getting into the preseason games—they played six back then, and they needed somebody to play running back.

We played San Francisco in the first preseason game at Kezar Stadium. They had to rush me to get me ready, and I wasn't sure when I would get a handoff versus a pitchout, so there were some uneasy moments. Actually, I ended up playing pretty well and they kept me at running back. Quite frankly, I had hoped to play tight end. Raymond Berry was the tight ends coach and being from Baltimore, I was a huge Berry fan. It was a thrill for me to work with him, and I enjoyed staying after practice and catching passes to work with Coach Berry, and, of course, Roger was always the guy throwing to me because he wanted the extra work, too.

GIL BRANDT *was among many who knew that even with the retirement of Meredith and the trading away of Jerry Rhome, Staubach would have his work cut out for him in competing against Craig Morton for the starting position. Let the quarterback controversy begin:*

Being a twenty-seven-year-old rookie was tough for Roger because Craig Morton was an extremely popular player. It's kind of like what took place this past year (2001) with the New England Patriots, with Tom Brady coming in to take over from Drew Bledsoe at quarterback. Bledsoe was a very popular player. If you keep both of them, you're going to have a split on your team because some of them are going to like one guy and the rest are going to like the other guy.

Quarterback controversies go back to the fifties with Bob Waterfield and Norm van Brocklin. Both were great quarterbacks on their way to the Hall of Fame, but there wasn't a coexistence between the two of them when they were together with the Los Angeles Rams. They had to make a decision: The Rams traded van Brocklin, and van Brocklin went on to win a world championship with the Philadelphia Eagles. Basically, we had to make the same kind of decision ultimately, and we did when we traded Morton, and Morton later took a team to the Super Bowl—the Denver Broncos—and Roger won two championships with the Cowboys.

It was very tough having both guys at quarterback. Nobody likes to be replaced, and nobody likes to see his friend pushed out. So, in essence, here's your Morton group and here's your Staubach group. When Landry talked to them, it wasn't sugarcoated, it wasn't what they wanted to hear, but he told them what was right. We finally traded Morton in the middle of the season (1972) because it wasn't a good situation.

You've also got to consider that your starting quarterback has to be getting about 90 percent of the reps in practice. Consequently, the number-one quarterback is happy and the number-two guy isn't happy. To a lesser degree, the number-one guy is also going to get more of the peripheral goodies, such as being on magazine covers.

Morton was a guy who was a quality guy and a smart person. But I don't think Morton was as focused as Roger was. Morton had great ability, but sooner or later you had to make a decision. You can't have a wife and a girlfriend, is what it amounts to. So Tom made the decision, and it turned out good for both teams. We won because we won the Super Bowl with Roger as starter and ended up getting Randy White with the pick we had acquired from the New York Giants in exchange for Craig, and Craig did well and got to the Super Bowl several years later with Denver and ended up with a good career.

Tom was very, very analytical in making decisions. For example, he had his staff chart *every* pass thrown in training camp—not just during scrimmages, but also during drills such as seven-on-seven or man-coverage drills. Any decision he made was based on

DALLAS COWBOYS

Staubach dropping back to pass, which always made systematic Cowboys head coach Tom Landry breathe a sigh of relief.

what took place, what the charts showed. Let's say Roger threw sixty out routes during training camp and completed twenty-seven, which is less than 50 percent, then Tom was smart enough to know that he wasn't going to throw a lot of out routes with Roger. Everything was planned down to the smallest detail. And Tom finally decided that if you're going to win, you have to have just one quarterback and hope that the guy holds up. Ironically, when Roger went down one time, Clint Longley took his place and won a game for us, and we ended up getting Tony Dorsett from the draft pick we acquired in eventually trading away Longley.

Staubach was not a stranger to Cowboys teammates when he finally showed up for good in 1969. He had taken "shore leave" in 1967 and 1968 to come to the Cowboys training camp. Linebacker LEE ROY JORDAN:

Roger could throw the ball really well. He would work out with us a week or two at a time, so we got a good feel for how strong an arm he had. This was a guy who wanted to make plays, and that excited a lot of people, because we knew it would give us a good continuation of good quarterbacks for a long time.

Meredith got us to where we could be a playoff and championship-caliber team, and then Craig filled the gap nicely there for a couple of years. Then Roger came along and performed extremely well in 1971, and we went on to win our first Super Bowl. That was the most confidence I had ever seen in the Dallas offensive coaching staff. They knew what they were going to do early on in preparing game plans, and there was no more changing things at the last minute—no indecision and second-guessing. With Duane Thomas, Calvin Hill, and Walt Garrison, we knew we were going to be able to run the football, and we knew that Roger would provide his share by completing a good percentage of his passes.

The coaches also knew we had a great matchup with our secondary against their receivers, that we could stop Miami's offense. I remember Coach Landry and his staff coming in during the first day of our pre-Super Bowl meetings and saying, "Here are the two defenses we're going to use against their receivers and their offensive team, and we're going to be able to beat them with these two coverages." It worked and we were able to force turnovers, something the Dolphins hadn't done much of during the year. We had a tremendous game both offensively and defensively against a very good football team.

TOM LANDRY:

Roger had spent a couple weeks of leave time at the Cowboys' training camps in '67 and '68. I had seen enough during those workouts to be impressed by his athletic ability and his arm. I'd even made an exception to one of my strictest policies and let him take a Cowboys' playbook to study one year when he had to return to active duty. We had also sent him some extra footballs when he was stationed in Vietnam so he could keep his arm in shape. But he was still a question mark. I would rather have had someone with two or three years of NFL experience as a backup to my new starting quarterback.[6]

GIL BRANDT *believes that Staubach's one-year tour in Vietnam paid football dividends, even if he wasn't actually fighting out in the jungle:*

To be a quarterback, it takes more than skill. It takes a person with mental toughness. I can only imagine that once you've seen bombs explode around you—like Roger did in Vietnam—then you acquire that mental toughness, if you don't already have it. You also need a guy with work habits, and obviously Roger had great work habits. The guy had the entire package of what you needed to be successful in the National Football League.

It doesn't make any difference what business you are in; the same rules apply. To be a good writer, a guy has to do a lot of research and have a lot of focus and flexibility in his thinking. It's highly unusual that you have as good an athlete and as competitive a person as you had in Roger, who came from a one-child family. I think if you were to do a comprehensive study of athletes in this world who have been successful, you're going to find that almost all of them have siblings.

"BULLET" BOB HAYES, *the 1964 Olympic gold-medal sprinter who once bore the tag "World's Fastest Human," was a football rarity, a predominantly track specialist who became a pass-receiving star in the NFL:*

Roger and I first met and got to know each other well when we played together for the College All-Stars in 1965. He hurt his shoulder scrambling against the Cleveland Browns. Most of the guys were rejoicing in the locker room after the game because we had come close to winning, but Roger sat in front of his locker with his head down. I went over to him and said, "Roger, do you have to go to the hospital? I'll be more than happy to go with you." He said, "No, thanks, Bob." But he has never forgotten my concern, and from that day on, when I needed help, he was there, just as I was for him. Of course, he's done a lot more for me than I ever could do for him.

I enjoyed knowing Roger in the All-Star Camp for three weeks, and then after he joined the Cowboys. He was not only a great quarterback, he had a presence about him. He's a real gentleman—even more of a straight arrow than his public image. Roger often wore a Fellowship of Christian Athletes T-shirt, and he always had a sense of pride and dignity about him in the way he walked and practiced. At first I didn't like the way he would always try to win a game by himself without the other players, but I later came to appreciate his burning desire to win.[7]

HAYES:

Roger went out of his way to relate to the black players, and sometimes it was comical. Once, we were playing cards in training camp, and Roger walked into Jethro Pugh's room when we were listening to a Temptations record. Roger said, "Oh, yeah, man, the Four Tops sure are good." He wanted us to know that he was hip. I said, "Roger, that's not the Four Tops; that's the Temptations." "Oh, sure, Bob," he answered, "it does sound like the Temps." Like I say, it was funny, but it also made us black players feel good because (at least) Roger was trying.[8]

Defensive end BOB LILLY *didn't regard Staubach in 1969 as a rookie:*

When he came to us he was immediately a team leader, even though he wasn't the starting quarterback. He was pretty rusty that first year in training camp. He was hard to trap, hard to catch, where Craig Morton had two bad knees. But as I recall, Roger wasn't very sharp with his passing in 1969.

Defensive tackle MIKE MCCOY, *while with the Green Bay Packers, faced off against Staubach a number of times during the seventies, including once when the game didn't really count . . . but it did:*

I'll never forget playing against Roger when I was a rookie with the Packers in 1970. It was just an exhibition game, but it was a really hot night and we were playing in the Cotton Bowl. I chased him all around all night and ended up getting leg cramps. You're pushing and pushing all night against all of these big offensive linemen trying to get to him, and he's back there scrambling all around.

He wasn't the same kind of scrambler that Fran Tarkenton was, where Tarkenton would be ten yards outside the hash marks and running around all over the place. Roger could hang between those hash marks and move around pretty well. Roger was what I would call "a pocket mover." He could take one or two steps to avoid the rush, step up or step back, or roll out two or three feet. He just had that knack for knowing how to move when you got close to him.

Even as a rookie, Staubach made it clear he wasn't content to bide his time on the bench. He wanted to start and didn't want to wait. TOM LANDRY:

Roger Staubach especially wanted to play. In one of our quarterback meetings, I talked about the importance of experience, pointing out that there wasn't a quarterback in the league who's ever won a championship with less than three years of experience. Even Joe Namath was in his fourth year before he won the Super Bowl.

At that Roger exploded. "How can you judge every individual by the same yardstick? If you do that, I don't have a chance to start because I'm only in my second year. You've got to judge every individual separately!"

A little taken aback by his outburst, I said, "Roger, see me after the meeting."

Then after everyone else left, I tried to explain my feelings about developing quarterbacks: How the mental knowledge of the game is so crucial in the pros. How I felt so many quarterbacks had been ruined and lost the confidence so essential to a good quarterback because they were sent in before they had the understanding needed to succeed against NFL defenses.

Roger wasn't convinced. "Coach," he said, "I feel I can physically make up for any mental shortcomings."

I wished Roger could be more patient. I had no doubts the necessary knowledge was going to come in time. He was not only intelligent but one of the most dedicated athletes I've ever known. If he gave his all, he knew he could succeed.[9]

Even though Landry had the Mount Rushmore countenance, STAUBACH *quickly discerned that there was an open mind behind the stone struggling to get out:*

At the end of the '69 season Landry sent out a lengthy questionnaire to all the players. He's a control-type person, and he was that way to the end, but he wanted more input into what to do. He was trying to send a message to say, "I can't do it all myself." And it was taken in the right vein. He wanted to know a lot of things, everything about the system, our opinion of the coaches.

Ermal Allen, who I thought was a very good coach, was moved from backfield coach. Jim Myers, the line coach, became the offensive coordinator. The one thing we didn't have for a long time, which I would have liked, was a quarterback coach. Ray Renfro used to help me as a coach, but he was a receiver. Landry would spend time with the quarterbacks, but during the game he was worried about the defense, and I'd come off the field and be talking to the other players, but it wasn't the same as talking to a quarterback coach. Later, Dan Reeves became that. I would have loved to have Dan involved earlier in my career.[10]

FRANK LUKSA, *at the time Staubach joined the Cowboys, was a beat writer and columnist for the* Fort Worth Star-Telegram. *He would later collaborate with Staubach on a book called* Time Enough to Win. *Luksa:*

Roger was an intense competitor with an enormous talent, as anyone could see, but he was also raw and a little bit rusty after four years in the service, even though he had played thirteen or fourteen games for a navy team down in Florida. As matters turned, Roger ended up starting his first game as a rookie, in Saint Louis, when Morton got hurt. The story goes that the night before the game, Staubach said to Tom Landry, "Just think: A year ago today I was the starting quarterback for the Pensacola Goshawks and we were playing Middle Tennessee State, and tomorrow I'm going to start against the Cardinals." Upon hearing this, Landry just rolled his eyes and walked off.

They wound up winning the game, 24-3. But that was pretty much the extent of Staubach's playing for the year, and for the next year as well, because Morton came back the following week and spent the rest of the season as the starting quarterback.

Morton was a terrific talent himself. The quarterback battle got pretty heated, especially after the Cowboys went to the Super Bowl (after the 1970 season) and lost to Baltimore, 16-13. Landry told Staubach going back on the plane that he would have every opportunity to compete for the number-one spot the next season.

That probably kept Roger from demanding a trade, because he was already getting close to being thirty years old and he wanted to play somewhere, or he felt he would just have wasted away.

Once the (1971) season began, it went back and forth between Roger and Morton, to the point where Landry, against Chicago, alternated them on every other play. It was like watching two ships passing each other in the night, back and forth, back and forth. The team was stumbling; their record was 4-3, and they weren't going anywhere because Tom couldn't make up his mind as to who to start. After they lost to Chicago, Landry finally named Staubach the starting quarterback, and they ran off ten straight victories the rest of the way and won Super Bowl VI, and Roger won the MVP.

Roger and Craig respected each other, but they weren't chummy. Roger didn't believe in being friends with someone he was competing against, but I didn't detect any friction between them either. Then Craig wound up being traded, which left Roger in charge, and that worked out well for both of them.

WALT GARRISON:

There always was a controversy with the Cowboys. When Eddie LeBaron was there, people were wanting Don Meredith; when Meredith was there they wanted Craig Morton; when Morton was there, they wanted Roger Staubach; and toward the end of Roger's time there, there were some people wanting Danny White.

Roger got mad at me one time after one of the L.A. papers asked me who the greatest quarterback was whom I had ever played with. I said Don Meredith, and that ticked Roger off, but he didn't hear the rest of the deal. I said that Meredith was probably the smartest quarterback I ever played with because he had a plan, and Tom Landry wasn't calling all the plays then. Don would run plays that would set up other plays. I also said the guy with the strongest arm was Craig Morton. But, I said, if you had the game on the line and you had to have one quarterback to take the last play, I said it would be Roger Staubach, because Roger Staubach is the best winner any time you play to win. But the paper didn't print all that.

That's true—Roger was a winner, and he still is. He could be down thirty points with two minutes to go and be thinking about how we were going to win, where the rest of us would be saying, "Where do you want to go eat?"

DAN REEVES *was amazed at Staubach's competitiveness and how it went well beyond the football field:*

Even in the weight room, he wanted to lift more reps than anyone else in there. It made him tougher. Roger lifted weights as much as anybody and it never affected his ability to throw the ball, and I've used that as an example over the years with other quarterbacks regarding their work habits. When we ran before practice, he wanted to be the first one across the finish line. Everybody saw those things in 1969 when he first reported.

I then became a player-coach in 1970. We had a good quarterback in Craig Morton, so it was a competitive situation. I never really looked at Roger as a project. We were playing together, and I admired the way he prepared himself.

I thought at the time Craig had a better grasp of what we were doing. He was the guy ready to do it, but Coach Landry saw in Roger the intangibles, such as leadership, that he had the vision to see. Most of the coaches were saying that Craig was the guy to go with, so you've got to give Coach Landry a lot of credit there. When he made that decision, it wasn't like any of us were adamantly against it. It was a can't-lose situation. In retrospect, he definitely made the right decision.

Both of those guys were very talented; it wasn't an easy decision to make. The thing that kind of swayed it to Roger, and there's no way to know this for sure, it was the leadership and stability that Roger embodied. You can't make anybody very focused, dedicated, or competitive like Roger was.

JERRY TUBBS, *on Staubach's readiness for the big time:*

He was always mature. I don't remember him ever being goofy. But you had to be pretty mature around Tom.

PETE GENT, *the former Dallas Cowboys wide receiver who would go on to write a "fictional" exposé of the Cowboys, entitled* North Dallas Forty, *never played alongside Staubach, but he reportedly said that Staubach would have been his pick if there had been a four-man race at quarterback:*

The only guy who ever had an effect on the Cowboys by being put into the game was Roger Staubach. Otherwise, every time Tom ever replaced a starting quarterback with a backup quarterback, he lost. And Craig (Morton) was probably the worst guy to ever put in, because Craig suffered from the same problem that coaches cited for why they never liked to let black guys play quarterback—'cause they always felt that black guys at quarterback would always throw long. That was their theory, like in basketball where they say the black guys never give up the ball. Well, that was the way Craig was. He'd get in and call three long passes, rather than try to work his way down the field.[11]

The Cowboys opened the 1969 season with six straight victories before getting abruptly stomped by the Browns in Cleveland, 42-10. It was not a fluke, for even after finishing the regular season with an 11-2-1 mark, the Cowboys went

*out in the first round of the playoffs, again losing to the
Browns, this time in Dallas, 38-14. There must have been
some funky carryover into the 1970 season, when the
Cowboys stumbled out to a 5-4 start. By this time Staubach,
for all practical purposes, was nailed to the bench. Even
though the Cowboys won five straight games to finish the season before advancing to the Super Bowl, the quarterback controversy continued to simmer. It only got worse after the
underdog Baltimore Colts upset the Morton-led Cowboys,
16-13, in Super Bowl V.* STAUBACH:

The way we started to win in '70 was a ferocious defense. Other
than the one game against the Houston Oilers, where Craig and
Bob Hayes had a fantastic game, we went into the playoffs really
with a defensive team. Because of Craig's injury, his confidence
was shot. *Sports Illustrated* ran a story that ours was a team without a quarterback. I was thinking, "I'm the backup quarterback.
This is really absurd." I was very confident I could play and perform. Though we had other players who were upset, I wasn't complaining, but once we hit the field our guys played hard, and that
last stretch our defense really got some momentum, but from my
perspective, with our great running game we should never have
lost that Super Bowl against Baltimore.[12]

*There was nothing like the occasional burst of good humor to
break the tension, and* BOB LILLY *recalls one humorous
episode at Staubach's expense:*

After practice at training camp, some of us guys would get together
in Walt Garrison's room, where he had this big wastebasket that was
used for dropping in pieces of wood while whittling. We would got
to Walt's room to dip snuff, drink beer, and whittle. I don't recall
Roger's drinking beer, but one day he decided that he would be one
of the boys and dip some snuff with us.

We had some Copenhagen, and Roger took it to read the label, which said "America's Finest Chewing Tobacco." You weren't supposed to actually chew the stuff, but Roger took what we called a double-finger wad of it, put it in his mouth, and started chewing on it. We then went to the team meeting, where we would always have a break after the first forty-five minutes. At that point, we heard Roger running down the hall and throwing up, and that's when we kind of fell in love with him. He was trying so hard to be one of the guys, and he had finally made it.

LEE ROY JORDAN *does his best to debunk Staubach's goody-two-shoes image:*

Roger wasn't a saint. He drank his beer and wine with the rest of us. But he was married to one woman and never looked for any others. That was the way he was raised, with his Catholic background. I assure you he turned down many opportunities to be a bad boy, and, no doubt about it, there were plenty of opportunities for celebrities of that stature to latch on to.

Sometimes George Allen and the Redskins would be quoted saying things about Roger that were intended to get him ticked off and too hyper for the game, but it never worked. I think they used Diron Talbert a few times with quotes in the paper to get Roger riled up. Most of the time it didn't affect Roger except to get him more motivated to win.

Defensive end LARRY COLE *added this little interesting tidbit about the life of Roger Staubach:*

The story I remember is the one about Craig Morton and this girl in the dorm during training camp in Thousand Oaks. Craig had been the backup to Don Meredith, and those guys were party animals. They always had the best women hanging around them. You've heard about the Cowboys being "Next Year's Champions." There wasn't a whole lot of seriousness about playing, and there usually was a party to go to. Roger changed that atmosphere once he got in.

Of course, it was an all-boys dormitory. This was on a Wednesday night, one of our nights out. Craig and some guys decided they were really going to surprise Roger. So they snuck this really good-looking young woman into the dorm. It was about ten-thirty or eleven o'clock at night and Roger was going to sleep just as everyone else was getting in. Anyway, with about five or six of us watching this whole thing, and everybody was trying to be real quiet, we got this girl to go to Roger's bed and start caressing him on his legs to see what would happen.

Roger woke up and, being quick-witted, he didn't miss a beat. He said, "Oh, hi. Would you like to see a picture of my wife and children?" That was so Roger. He won that battle, although he lost that battle with the snuff.

Back to the Landry System, as it pertains to offense. Let's turn it over to DAN REEVES:

Coach Landry was a defensive coordinator, so he liked devising things for the offense that he knew created problems for him from a defensive standpoint. Few coaches had a grasp of both like he did. The shifts, the linemen standing up—those were all specific things to distract the defense, to keep them from recognizing what you were going to do. All the formations, all the movement would create problems for the defense. Therefore, it made it very complicated.

His theory was that you could win games with a mediocre offensive team with a system, but the better the personnel, the better the system would be. At times before we became a really good offensive team, we were still a good offensive team because of the offense. Guys had to be really smart to learn the system. We had to eliminate some people if they couldn't achieve a certain test score.

In order for Staubach to truly fit into Landry's convoluted offense, he was going to have to exercise more discretion when it came to taking off with the ball, as REEVES *explains:*

DALLAS COWBOYS

Staubach getting his marching orders from above (in the coaches' box).

If Roger was going to improve as a quarterback, which he did, it was from not running at the first opportunity. Then when he did scramble, it was looking to make plays and not just for the sake of running. He improved on things like staying in the pocket and throwing the football—when things did break down, he learned the difference between having to run versus biding some time. He learned to read things and make throws on anticipation.

He was the most dedicated guy. He was never satisfied with his performance, and that was a joy to coach. And there was never any resentment; he wasn't one of those guys with real thin skin. He didn't get upset when you critiqued him.

When the 1971 season rolled around, the scenery hadn't changed much, except for the arrival of enigmatic yet super-talented running back Duane Thomas. Morton was still with

the Cowboys, and so was Staubach. The beat goes on, as
Dallas sports columnist SKIP BAYLESS *points out:*

Landry had given Staubach a brief chance midway through the season but had gone back to Craig Morton. Landry could change quarterbacks the way most coaches change expressions. Staubach was a little too hot-blooded for Landry—too quick to call an audible, bolt from the pocket, look for a secondary receiver. Staubach didn't grasp technical concepts quickly enough. He didn't always have the right answer in QB class. Staubach wasn't Landry's idea of the ideal quarterback-as-extension. Staubach was too confounded emotional and instinctive. He had the nerve to challenge Landry in quarterback meetings about why he wasn't getting a fair chance to win the job. Landry kept saying it takes every quarterback at least three years to learn the pro game. But Staubach didn't really have three years. He was already twenty-nine. After Super Bowl V he planned to ask Landry for a trade.[13]

One factor working against Staubach was the natural-born
leader's strong desire to call his own plays, which by the early
seventies was out of the question with Landry. The robotic-
quarterback concept was a source of frustration for Staubach.
Bayless often speculated that that particular beef might have
led to what many called Staubach's premature retirement
after the 1979 season. JERRY TUBBS:

Roger would have liked to call the plays, but that's just not the way our system worked, before Roger and after Roger. Tom controlled things. It's just like being in the navy—there's a chain of command. And Roger bought into that. Tom would listen to you—he could be very patient listening to you if you had a good point, but it didn't mean he was going to do anything about it. He was the ultimate authority. If you didn't buy into that, you weren't a professional.

*Seven games deep into the 1971 season, Landry went so far
as to alternate Morton and Staubach every play in a game
against the Chicago Bears. The result: Bears, 23-19. Once
again, the Cowboys were off to a ho-hum start, this time at
4-3.* CALVIN HILL *gives his take of what had transpired up to
that point, going back to his rookie year of 1969:*

When Morton came back in 1969, he was sensational, then he
hurt his shoulder. After that he continued to play, but he wasn't as
effective. He had a rifle for an arm, and that rifle didn't come back
the rest of the year. He struggled the next year because his motion
had been affected, and there were some throws he couldn't make.

Craig was hurting (late in 1970) and hadn't thrown particularly well all week (before Super Bowl V against Baltimore), and
to lose that Super Bowl the way we did, with Craig struggling,
Roger felt that if Coach Landry wasn't going to put him in in a situation like that, then time was running out for him with the
Cowboys as far as he was concerned. He had three children and
was twenty-eight years old, and his biological clock was running,
even though, athletically, he was young for his age.

When it got to the point where they were alternating quarterbacks every play or series (in 1971), it was particularly hard for
the receivers in terms of timing. Any quarterback controversy is
distracting. You want to be able to rally around one guy.

*When Landry announced in a team meeting that the two
quarterbacks would alternate plays starting against the Bears,*
STAUBACH *nearly fell out of his chair:*

I was sitting there, and I looked over at Morton, and he was looking at me, and I couldn't believe it. This was the most ridiculous
thing I ever heard of in my life. But Tom believed in his system. He

believed if he had two robots, it would work. What he was really saying was that he felt it didn't matter what player he was inserting into his system; if you did what he wanted you to do, you'd win. He didn't understand the emotion and the other human aspects, I don't think, of the notion that a person can make a difference, especially over a long season, and it may be in critical games.[14]

BOB LILLY:

Nobody wants to have two leaders. It can be especially difficult when it comes to calling signals at the line, because every quarterback has a different cadence. The rhythm is different. You can't get enough practice with both quarterbacks to be as crisp as you need to be. Landry's theory was that he wanted to have a quarterback for three years before he would start him. We wanted him to pick one quarterback, and we on defense wanted Roger because he was always messin' with us, which is something quarterbacks don't often do. I guess he made us feel good.

JERRY TUBBS, for one, liked the idea of a scrambling quarterback at the helm:

I always thought that helped win a Super Bowl. I know it did. That drives a defense crazy. When you have a guy with the ability to get away from the rush and then throw the ball down the field, like Roger could do, you could help your team immensely. Or, say it's third and four and your quarterback drops back to pass; he gets rushed and just like that—*ppphhhhttt!*—he's got five yards running, and the defense has to start all over again.

Fran Tarkenton was like that, and he was good enough quarterbacking a team that in turn was good enough to win the Super Bowl. Nine times out of ten, given four chances, Fran Tarkenton could have won a Super Bowl or two, but something would just keep happening along the way that he had no control over.

A lot of guys scrambled either because they couldn't read defenses or because they got "happy feet." Roger wasn't that way—he scrambled when he had to and when he knew it was the thing to do and that it would help his team.

A scrambling quarterback can be a killer, and that's Roger's forte. If he hadn't been able to run and scramble, he still would have been a good quarterback, but that ability to run and scramble put him over the top. And it's such an inspiration having a good quarterback who can come back and make that first down when there's a breakdown in blocking and everyone downfield is covered. A defensive back looks at this and says, "I have my man covered," and the defensive lineman says, "And, yeah, I finally made my escape," and then, *BOOM!* First down. The only drawback is that they get hurt more. That's what bothered Tom—he didn't like Roger doing a lot of running. Everything is a tradeoff.

Where other people called him "Roger the Dodger," I called him "Roger the Pocket" because they didn't want him to run. Roger believed in doing the right thing, but he would sometimes do things on his own. He wasn't just blindly obedient to every little thing that Tom wanted. That's the way Roger was—just like Captain Kirk from *Star Trek*—a great leader with charisma and yet respectful, who sometimes just says to heck with the regulations if following regulations to the letter meant putting his own crew in danger.

Longtime defensive back PAT RICHTER, *who spent much of his career playing with the Washington Redskins, joined the Cowboys in 1971, near the end of his career. Richter:*

The difference between Roger and Fran Tarkenton was that you felt if you could at least keep Tarkenton in the area of the pocket, you could contain him and limit his effectiveness. With Roger in the pocket, it didn't hurt him at all. He was as effective still in the pocket as he was running out. Because Roger was a little bigger person (than Tarkenton), he could actually run a little better, being somewhat harder to bring down, and Roger could throw on the run when he had to.

I played a number of years with Sonny Jurgenson, and even roomed with him for a while. He didn't look like a great athlete, but he was. And he was the classic dropback pocket passer. He could really zip it and he could also lay the ball out there really soft as well as any quarterback could.

I understand that Tom Landry didn't allow Roger to call his own plays. But having been with the Cowboys for even such a short time, I could see that it was a very complicated offensive system. What Sonny was so good at was being able to sense things, to sense the timing and the feel of a game sort of from a cat-and-mouse-type mentality. I thought Roger had the ability to do that, too.

LEE ROY JORDAN *had these insights about the relationship between Landry and Staubach, which helps explain why Staubach could never really crack the code of what it took to be Landry's quarterback confidante:*

Roger's great leadership was by example, by showing everybody how hard to work and how enthusiastic to be about every play. I think he and Coach Landry had a good relationship in that regard, but it wasn't a tight one. Tom wasn't tight with anyone. That's just the way Tom was. It had been a similar deal with Don Meredith. I don't think Roger ever developed the rapport with Coach Landry that he had wished for, just like Don, Craig, or any of us had been unable to do. I think Tom, down deep, felt he couldn't be friends with players and still make tough personnel decisions and those kinds of things. His style of management was keeping his distance.

Tom wouldn't even develop a father-son kind of rapport with his players that would have allowed him to maintain a level of respect while still being accessible. That was too difficult for him. I think all of the quarterbacks wanted that and worked for it from their side, but Tom wasn't able to reciprocate.

After the lackluster 4-3 start in 1971, the Cowboys pulled it all together once again. They ran the table the rest of the way, winning seven in a row before knocking off Minnesota, 20-12, and San Francisco, 14-3, to earn a return trip to the Super Bowl, this time against the Miami Dolphins in New Orleans. No more talk about Next Year's Champions: Dallas won, 24-3. Duane Thomas rushed for ninety-five yards, and Staubach won game MVP honors after completing twelve of nineteen passes for 119 yards and two touchdowns. BOB LILLY:

We went into that game pretty confident even though, from watching films from a defensive standpoint, we could see that the Dolphins executed better on offense than any team we had seen since the Green Bay Packers in the sixties. They didn't make many mistakes—they didn't fumble and they didn't throw the ball away. I don't think (fullback Larry) Csonka had fumbled the ball all season.

Jim Kiick could do a number of things, but when they had Mercury Morris in there we were scared to death because he had such blazing speed and was so elusive. Plus they had a great offensive line, and they had Paul Warfield, who was one of the best wide receivers I ever played against. They could do it all with Bob Griese at quarterback—go deep with the ball or play the three-yards-and-a-cloud-of-dust type of offense.

We had won nine games in a row going in, so we were pretty positive. We had a little dissension on the team because Duane (Thomas) didn't talk, but by then it didn't really matter.

As for the game itself, it was a nice, cool day to play football. The first thing I remember is that I expected there to be a majority of Dallas Cowboys fans there, but that wasn't the case. The stadium was extremely loud, and it was like we were playing inside a drum. We had to go to a pretty simple cadence calling signals.

We held them to three points. We forced some turnovers and didn't let their ground game get out of hand. Roger did a great job scrambling around and finding people in the end zone. We just didn't make any errors. We ran the ball pretty well, and that was important because we did well in keeping the ball out of the hands of Miami's offense.

WALT GARRISON:

Our whole goal at the start of the (1970) season had been to get to the Super Bowl, and when we did win to get there, we had a letdown because then we were feeling that we had already accomplished our goal for the season. The next year our goal was to win the Super Bowl, and we did against Miami.

That win over Miami was probably the most perfect game I had ever been a part of, both offensively and defensively. I remember Miami not being able to do anything—our defense was unbelievable—and everything Coach Landry put into the offensive plan worked. We keyed off the middle linebacker, and I ran the ball a lot in the first half to cut back against the grain because Nick Buoniconti was very fast and covering the outside and the off-tackle holes. In the next half, we faked the ball with me going inside, and pitched the ball out to Duane (Thomas) going to the outside.

It seemed like we didn't make any mistakes, except for the time that Calvin Hill fumbled the ball on their two-yard line. Without that, the score probably would have been 31-3.

What I remember about the dressing room is that a lot of people were happy, but they weren't *that* happy. I don't know how to explain it—it was more quiet resolve that we had finally done it and now we could relax. It wasn't one of those pop-the-champagne-cork moments where everybody sprays everybody else.

JERRY TUBBS:

After we won the Super Bowl, somebody asked me what it felt like to finally win it all, and I told them it's kind of like being constipated for a long time and then finally having a bowel movement. It was more of a relief than it was exhilaration.

In '66 we had gotten to the playoffs, in '67 we had lost in the Ice Bowl to Green Bay, in both '68 and '69 we had gotten knocked out by Cleveland in the first round, and then in '70 we got all the way to the Super Bowl before losing. It was great and it was fun when we finally won the Super Bowl (beating the Miami Dolphins in Super Bowl VI, 24-3), but by the same token it was a load off our shoulders. Every year before that we had been known as "Next Year's Champions."

I can even remember how as far back as 1963 or 1964 we had been on the cover of *Sports Illustrated*, as an up-and-coming team—supposedly—even though we hadn't won anything yet. But they could *see* that someday we were going to be there. We were making progress, and that showed in '65 when we went to the Runner-up Bowl, or the Playoff Bowl, which is what they called it at that time. In '66 we finally went to a playoff game with winners, but it still took us a number of years after that to get to the top, even going backward in '68 and '69 considering what we had done in '66 and '67 (making it to the NFL Championship Game before losing, both times, to the Green Bay Packers).

We wanted to win and the press was on us with all this "Next Year's Champions" talk and all that crap. We were winning and were considered a loser, basically. That's the way it goes when you reach a certain plateau of winning and then don't win at all—you're labeled a loser. I remember one time, I think it was after the '80 or '81 season, we went all the way to the NFC Championship Game and lost to the Rams. Soon after that, as I was going up to my ranch in McKinney one day, I met this lady who liked football but wasn't real knowledgeable, and she said to me, "What's wrong with y'all?" That was typical of the way people thought because we had been winning so much. There we were, one of the last four teams playing that season out of twenty-eight in the league, meaning we were in the upper echelon, but yet we were perceived as losers.

Winning Super Bowl VI was a crowning achievement for Staubach, but he still had some work in front of him before anyone dared call him Captain America. First of all, Morton was still around in 1972, leading the Cowboys back into the playoffs with a 10-4 mark, while Staubach nursed a shoulder injury most of the year. Two days before Christmas, however, the Cowboys played the San Francisco 49ers in a divisional playoff game that would change Staubach's life forever. The king of the fourth-quarter comeback was born. Staubach came off the bench in the fourth quarter with the Cowboys trailing, 28-13. Roger the Dodger led the Cowboys to the come-from-behind 30-28 victory, throwing touchdown passes to Billy Parks and Ron Sellers in the final minute and a half, sandwiched around a successful Toni Fritsch onside kick.
WALT GARRISON *recalls:*

That was out at Candlestick Park. They were beating us up and down the field. Dick Nolan was the 49ers coach, and he had put in a lot of stuff to stop our offense and they had some things to run against our Flex defense, and it was working.

When we lined up to kick the onside kick, I'm thinking, *There ain't no way we're going to recover an onside kick.* Toni Fritsch, our placekicker, kicked the ball behind his back—he was actually offside because his right foot was in front of the ball and he kicked it behind his right foot with his left foot, and kicked it over to the right instead of kicking it over to the left. We (Mel Renfro) recovered it and went down and scored. It was unbelievable.

Roger never quit, and that game was a good one. That game pretty much signaled the end of our quarterback controversy. You can still ask Roger today about the fact that he didn't play in the Super Bowl game that we lost to Baltimore, and he still thinks we could have won had he been playing quarterback, and I'm not sure that he's wrong.

LEE ROY JORDAN *was there, too:*

Everything started to click when they put Roger in: Roger started making throws that were unbelievable, and we had receivers making great catches. The 49ers thought they had the game won and had started taunting us from the sideline, saying stuff like, "How does it feel to be the ones getting beat this time?" We had beaten them several times in a row in the playoffs, and they felt like they were getting revenge for that.

But Roger kept us coming back, and then we got the onside kick. Three plays later—*BOOM!*—it's a touchdown and we win.

The confidence that Roger had was unbelievable. He believed he could get the job done just given the opportunity. From that time on, Coach Landry knew that Roger would be our starting quarterback. On the other hand, I don't know if anybody could have taken Craig's place had he not gotten hurt. The guy was unbelievable—a smart quarterback who could read defenses extremely well, and he had a rocket for an arm. If Craig hadn't gotten hurt, Roger might have ended up playing for someone other than the Cowboys. There was a stretch of about eight games in 1970 where I thought Craig was about as good a quarterback as I had ever seen play the game. You feel bad for Craig that he didn't get to fulfill that opportunity, but you also have to look at it as a great opportunity for Roger.

Sportswriter FRANK LUKSA *was also at Candlestick that day:*

Roger came in and led them to the miracle comeback win over San Francisco, but then the Cowboys lost badly to Washington in the NFC Championship game. That was when the Redskins' Diron Talbert started his war of words against the Cowboys, saying that they "had started the wrong quarterback." It was a remark Staubach never forgot or forgave. As captains later on, they would meet at midfield before the game and refuse to shake hands with one another.

There were some doubts that BOB LILLY *would be able to play against the 49ers because of back problems:*

I got there late to the game because my back had gone into spasms during practice the week before the game and I had been in the hospital. I had about fifty-eight shots of Novocain, and I played the first quarter—not very well, but I was out there.

We had recently beaten the 49ers in some other playoff games, and some of them were doing things I had never seen before, like giving Coach Landry the finger as they went by our bench and calling us "Losers." We figured we had nothing to lose when we fell way behind, and when we came back to beat them, that destroyed them.

The sight I remember most from that game after it was over was our guys, like Larry Cole, rolling around on the ground in celebration. I would have been doing it, too, had it not been for my back. I could barely stand up.

MIKE MCCOY *never played with the Cowboys, and he passed up a chance to play one in the movie version of* North Dallas Forty, *which came out in 1979. McCoy talks about the movie, why he skipped his screen test, and how the flick depicted Staubach:*

I helped John Matuszak get a role in the movie. I was in my office up in Green Bay one February, and I get a call from Tom Fears, the former coach, who was consulting on the movie. They wanted a couple big ol' redneck guys for a couple of roles, and they were going to offer me more money than I made playing football that year.

When I told my wife that I was going to go down to Texas to read for one of the roles, she said, "Have you read the book?" I said, "Well, uhh, not really, but as I understand they're not going to be as bad with it on screen as they were in the book (in terms of the R-rated nature of the book)." She said, "Okay, in fifteen years do you want your kids to see their dad in a movie like that?" I realized it wasn't worth it. So when Tom (Fears) called me back, I suggested John Matuszak. They got ahold of him and had him read for the part. It turned out that they liked him so much that they expanded his role in that movie. He was a natural.

The movie depicted Roger as this really religious guy who was wimpy, and Roger's totally the opposite of a wimp. It was pathetic. I'm so glad I didn't get involved with the movie. What bothers me is how so many gullible people can look at all these Hollywood movies and take them as gospel truth. The thing about it, you never heard Roger say anything about that movie. He just went about his business. He's a smart guy.

While North Dallas Forty was viewed as a knock against Tom Landry's cold-hearted ways and the irreverent side of the Cowboys' collective character, the movie actually worked to add color and depth to the Cowboys' public image.
WALT GARRISON:

I'm not sure we had a lot of character; we had a lot of characters. A lot of times a lot of different personalities will fit well together on a team, and we did. I don't think everybody on the team can be super-serious about football because then it would be pretty boring.

There were guys there who were fun-loving, and there were other guys who took the game very seriously. If you went into our locker room before a game, some guys would be laughing and joking, some would be playing dominoes, some would be over in a corner by themselves, and others would be slapping lockers around and crap like that—it takes all kinds of personalities to make up a winning team. Roger never was one to play dominoes or laugh a lot; he was pretty serious about football, and that's the way he was before a game. He didn't go around pep-talking everybody or anything like that. He was pretty quiet while having to go back over all this game-plan stuff that, thank God, I didn't have to remember.

JERRY TUBBS:

Tom made some compromises in there, and we won the Super Bowl (against Miami). Duane (Thomas) used to frustrate Dan Reeves so. In a meeting he would ask questions to test the players, and when he asked Duane, Duane would just say, "The answer's in the (play)book." Tom could get away with letting things slide for a little while, but he wasn't going to put up with it forever. Duane did go to all the practices and he did work out, but he was just hard to get along with. There were few teams in the league that didn't have problems like that, though, and it was a tribute to Tom and Roger, as leaders, that they were able to work through those problems.

Even the names gracing the Dallas roster in the seventies had a certain kind of Hollywoodish, roughneck Cowboy charm to them—Jethro Pugh, Butch Johnson, Billy Joe DuPree, Golden Richards, Blaine Nye, Lee Roy Jordan, D. D. Lewis, Charlie Waters, Bob Lilly, and on and on. FRANK LUKSA:

This team had more characters than anybody in the league. You had a world-class soccer player in Toni Fritsch, who had been found on a kicking caravan; Walt Garrison, who for his signing bonus wanted, and got, a horse trailer; Ed "Too Tall" Jones, who quit football for a while to become a professional boxer; Cornell Green, who had never played football in college—he was a basketball player; several players from then-obscure colleges, such as Cliff Harris

DALLAS COWBOYS

Roger the Dodger heading upfield against the Philadelphia Eagles.

from Ouachita Baptist and Rayfield Wright from Fort Valley State; and a best-selling author in Pete Gent, who wrote *North Dallas Forty*—which illustrates the success of the Cowboys because you never heard of a best-seller called *North Cincinnati Forty* or *North Atlanta Forty*.

You also had a lot of guys with a penchant for self-deprecating humor, such as Larry Cole, the defensive end, who intercepted four passes in his career, and they were all against the Washington Redskins. He intercepted three early in his career, and then there was something like a ten-year gap before he got his last one. I asked Cole after the game, "How do you explain the ten-year gap in interceptions?" to which he replied, "Anyone can have an off-decade."

◇

By the early seventies, the Cowboys-Redskins rivalry had
started to reach another level of intensity, with George Allen
taking the reins soon after Vince Lombardi's death. Allen
brought in veterans from around the league to give the
Redskins a quick infusion of ready-made talent, which
included linebacker MYRON POTTIOS. Pottios talks about
chasing Staubach on the field and battling Dallas in the
standings:

Roger put a lot of defensive pressure on you because of his ability to run as well as to pass. Defensive linemen had to chase him,
and there's nothing more tiring than chasing a scrambling quarterback all over the place. As a linebacker, you don't know when
to leave your guy because you're not supposed to leave him until
Roger crosses the line of scrimmage, so there you are sticking
with your guy while Roger is going all over the place, and now
your guy is breaking his pattern. That creates a tremendous
amount of pressure.

Roger was a great runner and a great competitor, and he just
never quit. Plus there was the fact that there was a rivalry between
the Redskins and the Cowboys. From our standpoint we knew we
had to beat these guys to win our division, and vice versa. It also
was a situation where (Redskins head coach) George Allen helped
create interest in the game. He would get us pumped up by making derogatory statements about the Cowboys. Diron Talbert was
the most outspoken guy among the players because George Allen
was telling him to say those things. He also thought it might affect
the Cowboys' minds, too.

We didn't *hate* the Cowboys. There were a bunch of other
teams in the league we needed to be concerned with beating. You
have to be prepared no matter who you're playing. The only reason that game was more controversial was because it was played
up so much in the media. It was played up by the media as well as
the coaches—more George Allen than Tom Landry, of course.

*The 1973 season was a turning point in Staubach's career. In
came free agent DREW PEARSON, who would soon become
Staubach's favorite all-time receiver:*

The way I came through Dallas trying to project a positive image
for myself is what I learned from Roger and what I took from him.
I always said to myself, "If I leave this game without any money,
but if I have my name intact, I could do something with that after
my playing days are over." Well, I left this game with no money,
and I had to rely on my name after everything was over, and it's
paid off for me. Some players even label me "the black Roger
Staubach." They say that Roger was the guy Landry talked to
when he wanted to get to the white players. I was the guy Landry
talked to when he wanted to get to the black players. . . . I worked
to make it happen that I was respected and looked upon in that
same light. So Roger and I, because of that, we got along great.[15]

*PEARSON takes us back to his free-agent days starting out
with the Cowboys and the key role Staubach played in making
him feel at home:*

Roger played a big role in making it happen for me, or at least in
giving me an opportunity that turned into an extended look. He
noticed some potential in me when I came down for some of the
minicamps.

After graduating from Tulsa in May, I moved down to Dallas,
and Roger and I would spend many hours together on the practice field working out. Here I was, an undrafted rookie out of the
University of Tulsa, and there's the legendary Roger Staubach,
pretty much taking me under his wing in the sense that he threw
the ball for me, letting me run routes for him. He would run me
until my tongue was hanging out. He would ask me if I was okay,
and I'd say, "Yes, sir." No way was I going to let him know that I
was tired.

We would get together at about eight or nine in the morning and go until about eleven or eleven-thirty. That would give me enough time to shower and grab something to eat before heading out to my other job.

In doing that, he saw something in my ability, and he approached the Cowboys on my behalf. I would work out with him in the morning. Then, because I was married, I would go to my part-time job in the afternoon with Merchants Van Lines loading eighteen-wheeler trucks with all kinds of items, ranging from clothes to caskets to refrigerators. You do that in Dallas between one and five o'clock in the afternoon in the summer, and inside those trucks it was like a sauna every day out there, hours at a time. It was tough work. After that, I'd go back home and then do my evening workout, which was going out to run for my conditioning and endurance.

I would be dragging a bit in the morning, and Roger noticed all this. He finally asked me what I was doing, and after I told him about my part-time job, he went to Gil Brandt and said, "Would you help this guy out, because he's got some potential, and he should be out here on the practice field instead of loading trucks."

As it was, I was tripping out while all this was going on, having a Dallas Cowboys T-shirt on while wearing a pair of Mel Renfro shoes and catching passes from Roger Staubach. The reason we had that time together in June was because in those days NFL veterans would usually take that time of year off to go on vacation with their family before training camp. So a lot of the other guys weren't around. That's why Roger and I always had so much time to work out together. One thing I never did was ask Roger why *he* wasn't on vacation, too, like all the other veterans. He might have taken it later because we didn't have to be at training camp until the third week in July.

After Roger went to Gil Brandt asking if the Cowboys could help me out, they gave me five hundred dollars a month, which was enough money to allow me to quit my part-time job and spend more time at the practice field. Because the Cowboys made that kind of investment in me, they gave me a longer look in training camp. They certainly wanted to get their money's worth out of me. They were patient with me, even after the veterans returned and I was lagging behind them a bit in developing as a player.

PEARSON *details those two-man workout sessions with the seemingly tireless Staubach:*

We'd just run some general routes, working a lot on timing—the quick sideline, the deep sideline, the end route, the post pattern, and those kind of things. Then we would add some spice to the workouts by simulating game-type situations. So after every pass, I would jog back to him as though going back to a huddle, just like you would in a game. We would even lean over with hands on our knees as in a real huddle to discuss the next play.

Most of these plays were foreign to me because I hadn't gotten the playbook yet and didn't know the terminology, but he would explain all that to me in our own little huddle. As we broke the huddle, he would tell me what route to run. I would go out there and line up, and he might tell me that I should line up a little tighter or perhaps a little wider, depending on the particular situation. I would then run the route and catch the ball. We'd go down the entire length of the field before scoring a touchdown and then start over on a whole new series of passes.

We always ended each workout by throwing the deep ball, either the deep post or the deep streak down the sideline. He would throw it forty, fifty, sixty yards, and I would make the catch and run it into the end zone. He would jog down the field behind me, I would catch my breath, and then we'd do it going in the other direction. We had it established that we wouldn't leave the field until we had completed our last pass. So if I dropped a pass or he overthrew me, we would run it over and over until I got it right.

For a guy like that to be out there with me was invaluable for me in terms of gaining the confidence that I could play at that level. There would sometimes be a few people out there watching us from over the fence, but the right people knew that I was out there with Roger, and the right people were Tex Schramm, Gil Brandt, and Tom Landry.

The first thing that struck me was his ability to throw the football so hard. I threw it hard when I played quarterback for two seasons at Tulsa before moving to receiver, and the quarterbacks who threw to me at Tulsa didn't throw anything nearly as hard as this. He could really bring it.

The other thing I noticed was his natural ability as a quarterback. This guy was a pro in all respects: his attitude, his mannerism, his work ethic. I was getting a lesson on the spot as to how to be a pro and how to learn the flow of the game.

PEARSON *raves on:*

He was football's version of a gym rat. But his athletic abilities were more man-made than they were God-given talent, although he had a lot of intangibles about him that were God-given. Add his competitive nature to that great work ethic, and you had a tremendous athlete. He was inspired to work out all the time.

When I first came through in 1973, this was about the time that teams were starting to have minicamps and all these off-season conditioning programs. Coach Landry had to have a leader to inspire all this new stuff and accept it. Roger was that guy. He accepted it, and the other guys just fell in line. Because I ended up playing with him for seven years, I came to understand that he was the guy who set the tone and tempo for what the rest of the team did, not just the guys on offense.

Pearson eventually played eleven seasons with the Cowboys, 1973 through 1983, seven of those with Staubach. The continuity paid off. PEARSON:

Over time we could pretty much read each other's minds in games. Many times I would come back to the huddle, and Roger would be looking at the ground while talking to me so he wouldn't give it away to the defense that he was talking to me.

He might say, "What's that guy doing to you out there? Can you get inside of that cornerback? Can you run that end route? If he's overplaying inside, can you get outside?" Those things developed over time. The work we did together before I joined the team was nothing compared to the work we did after we were actually teammates.

Even when I was a rookie, he would be asking me all these questions, and by his seeing me work so hard he developed a lot of confidence in me. Later, as we developed, we'd come out of a huddle with a play called and he would give me that certain look, and I knew what he meant. I knew that he wanted to come to me and that he wanted me to run a particular route. A certain kind of nod or a lifting of his head would convey to me a particular route that he wanted me to run. Sometimes he would just use his fingers, showing me the number nine as we came to the line, and he knew that the cornerback had no idea what that nine meant. I can tell you now—the nine referred to the streak route down the sideline.

Coach Landry knew all about this improvisation, that we had these senses about stuff going on. He would let us take liberties with the plays, especially when we were in the two-minute drill. Of course, if we hadn't had success with that, Coach Landry would have had a problem with what we were doing on our own, you can be sure of that.

CALVIN HILL *left the Cowboys after the 1974 season to jump to the World Football League, ending his six-year Cowboys association with Staubach that sometimes carried with it the additional duty of Staubach consoler:*

When you think of great competitors and having the will to win, you think of people like Michael Jordan or Michael Irvin who came along later with the Cowboys. Roger hated to lose—he was the worst loser I've ever seen in my life. When we lost a game, he took it personally.

There were times I would get a call from Marianne telling me that Roger was really down in the dumps. So I would go over there to talk to him. I would remind him that "you don't take all of the credit when we win, so why do you takes all the blame when we lose?" Still, losing left a bitter taste in him.

Losing is a terrible feeling. He was willing to do whatever it took to win. Lots of people have the will to win, but do they have the will to prepare to win? Roger did.

One of the toughest wins to prepare for was the Cowboys' game at Saint Louis in their last regular-season game of 1973. Staubach's mom, Betty, died less than a week before the contest, following a prolonged battle with cancer. Betty Staubach spent much of the last few months of her life living with Roger and Marianne and their family in Dallas before returning to Cincinnati after Thanksgiving. She passed away on December 13, a Thursday. Roger made her funeral arrangements that day, went to practice, flew to Cincinnati on Friday for funeral services on Saturday, then caught a plane to Saint Louis for the game that Sunday. He completed fourteen of nineteen passes for 256 yards and three touchdowns, nailing down his second league passing title. The Cowboys won, 30-3. DREW PEARSON:

To this day, Roger is a special kind of a guy. Talk about thick skin, there is no question he had that. His parents raised him with a lot of discipline, and so in doing that, he's been taught a lot of the values you really need. Roger is the type of teammate, even though this tragedy happened in his life, he knew that his mother wanted him to continue to go out there and play. He didn't want his anguish, his grief, his problems to become our problems, and that's just the kind of guy he was.[16]

After beating Saint Louis, Dallas defeated the Los Angeles Rams, 27-16, in a divisional playoff before losing to Minnesota, 27-10, in the NFC Championship game. Staubach by this time was well-entrenched as the Cowboys' number-one quarterback, although Morton still was hanging around. Not for long. Six games deep into the 1974 season, Morton was traded to the New York Giants. By then the Cowboys were 2-4 and on their way to missing the postseason for the first time since 1964. So, this is as good a time as any to bring up again the play-calling controversy, now that the quarterback controversy was over. Turn it over to TOM LANDRY:

For years we (Staubach and Tom) had a running conflict over the issue of play calling. When Roger first established himself as the Cowboys' number-one quarterback, I let him call his own plays on the field. But during the '73 season, I reassumed play-calling duties, shuttling the plays in with a substitute on every play. While I didn't explain my reasons at the time, I made the decision in part as an attempt to take some of the emotional pressure off Roger during the time his mother was dying of cancer. But the fact was I always preferred calling the plays from the sidelines. . . .

I remember one game in '78 when I called a short pass to fullback Robert Newhouse. But instead of dumping the ball off short, Roger sent Drew Pearson deep on a post pattern. Just as he released the ball, a blitzing linebacker rang Roger's bell, splitting his lip, and ending his play for the day with a dizzying concussion. The pass fell incomplete, and Danny White had to come in and finish the game. Afterwards in the locker room, I walked over to check on Roger and his bleeding lip. "You know, Roger," I said, trying not to smile, "for a while, every time you look in the mirror to shave, you're gonna have a reminder *not* to change my plays."

But Roger got his digs in, too. One day as he came off the field following an interception, I met him at the sidelines, asking, "Why did you throw that pass? The defensive man had him covered."

Roger snapped right back, "Why did you call such a ridiculous play?"

We lived with this underlying tension between us for so long that we could joke about it.[17]

STAUBACH:

I always wanted to call the plays because I would have been a very good player to control things on the field. I was not a brilliant reader of defenses. Craig was much more in the mold of what Coach Landry wanted at quarterback, and Danny (White) was much more of a scholar of the game. The coaches would ask me to get up at the blackboard and show a blocking scheme, and I'd kid around and drive 'em crazy. I just knew instinctively.

If we'd had an offensive coordinator calling the plays who worked closely with the quarterbacks all week, that would have been different. But Coach Landry controlled everything, and he and I didn't really have any dialogue until Saturday night when he'd call me up to go over the game plan.[18]

FRANK LUKSA, *veteran sportswriter, weighs in with his assessment of the play-calling snafu:*

Roger accepted the system as it existed. That's the way things were done. Obviously, he would have liked to have called plays, and if he had, he probably would have thrown ninety passes a game. Over the years, I think he and Landry got to thinking a lot alike when it came to the offensive game plan.

Every Saturday night before a home game, at a particular

hour, Roger would go into his study, get his playbook ready, and sit there, and at exactly the same time the phone would ring and it would be Landry. When Roger answered the phone, Landry wouldn't even introduce himself. He would just start talking about minor adjustments that they were going to make.

Roger didn't agree with every play that Landry called, but he didn't make a big show of resistance about it. He tried to work with it. Landry would come to him and ask, "What are you comfortable with? Do you like this? Do you like that?" and he would usually defer to what Staubach was most comfortable with. From that standpoint, they had a good relationship.

When 1975 arrived, Staubach's seventh season with Dallas, it marked the first time that Staubach went to training camp without having to think about Morton. Any boredom was short-lived, however, as along came a rookie by the name of THOMAS "HOLLYWOOD" HENDERSON, who quickly learned the rules when it came to scrimmaging against Staubach— hands off:

I almost got fined for sacking Roger Staubach. We were having a blitzing drill, the running backs standing in the backfield trying to protect the quarterback while the linebackers coming full-blast had to run over or around them to get to him. . . . When you get to the quarterback you're supposed to stop. Not me. I went and hit him, got the coaches' attention. Landry about fell out of his tower. "I forgot to tell you men," he called through his bullhorn, "you don't hit Roger Staubach. You don't hit the quarterback." Hell, I was disappointed.[19]

Henderson's disappointment soon faded. The Cowboys rebounded from their 8-6 season of a year earlier to go 10-4

and win their way back into the Super Bowl, where they lost,
21-17, to Terry Bradshaw and the Pittsburgh Steelers.
HENDERSON:

Roger Staubach was just about perfect that season. We weren't putting anybody away; most of our games were close and down to the wire. A lot of times it just blew our minds that we'd won. We had an aging defense backed up by some raging rookies. We knew that if we could hold them close till the fourth quarter with two minutes to go, Staubach would win it for us. If we needed a touchdown, he got it. If we needed a field goal, he'd run the ball to where the kicker, Toni Fritsch, liked it. Right hash mark? He'd put it over there. Left hash mark? Sure. Right in the middle of the field? Sure, Toni, here it is. Now kick it.[20]

Dallas had won its first four games in 1975 before hosting the
Green Bay Packers who, under first-year head coach Bart
Starr, had lost their first four games. Packers defensive tackle
MIKE MCCOY *remembers that game well:*

We went down there and beat them, 19-17. That was a big win for us because Bart was under pressure right away after having taken over for Dan Devine, who had gone to Notre Dame.

One of the things I remember about that 19-17 game was that I had a big fight with Randy White. I had the dubious distinction of being the captain of the wedge on the kickoff-return team. That's the guy who had the responsibility of watching the kicked ball go into the hands of the return man, and then turn around to face upfield and say, "Go!"

The kicking team always had one guy coming down with a forty-yard head of steam to hit the wedge head-on, and that guy for the Cowboys was Randy White. I think he was rookie that year. We had a pretty good collision, and then on the second collision I put an arm into his head and we went down to the ground, scratching and clawing at each other until the referees came in and broke it up.

What was interesting is that I didn't know Randy and never saw him during the off-season. But one year I was at a banquet in Elmira, New York, just after he had made the Hall of Fame. He's sitting up there and sees me in the audience, and he says, "Mike, how ya doin'? I remember that fight. I shouldn't have picked on you. I was just a rookie."

No mention of the Cowboys' 1975 season would be complete without recalling the Hail Mary game, in which Staubach hit Drew Pearson for a fifty-yard touchdown pass in the final seconds to beat the Minnesota Vikings, 17-14, in a divisional playoff at Minnesota. FRANK LUKSA, *the sportswriter, almost missed the play, preparing for what apparently was the inevitable Cowboys loss:*

All this happened as I was standing up and about to leave the press box to start heading down to the locker room to talk to the Cowboys about the loss.

There were a lot of weird things about that game. After Pearson caught that fourth-down pass and was ruled inbounds after being pushed out by a defensive back, as he was lying there, a security guard kicked at him. Then came the Hail Mary, which I thought was going to be called back because there was a flash of yellow that went past Pearson as he caught the ball. It turned out to be a tennis ball thrown by a fan out of the stands.

Some crazy things happened after the ensuing kickoff. Somebody threw a whiskey bottle out of the end-zone seats and hit the umpire flush in the head, knocking him out cold. The epitaph of the game was our finding out, after the game, that Fran Tarkenton's father, a Methodist minister down in Atlanta, had died during the game. The weird part was that his father's first name was Dallas.

People in Minnesota felt that this was the best team they had around that time, even though they had four other teams go to the Super Bowl. They claim that Drew Pearson pushed off on Nate Wright on the Hail Mary pass, but I've watched the replay about a dozen times since then and I don't see it.

DREW PEARSON *offers his recollections of the game:*

It had been a strange game. Mostly, it was the whole situation of being in the playoffs as a wild-card team and playing a Minnesota Vikings team that had been the best in the league and probably better than any of their four other teams that went to the Super Bowl.

It was an overcast day; cold, about ten degrees. The stadium was old and ratty, and you were dressing on top of each other in the locker room. You come out of the tunnel and into this old stadium; you look to the right and you see this baseball diamond, with the stands way off behind the first-base line. Then you look to the left and you see these short bleachers with both teams' bench areas on the same side of the field. You say to yourself, "Is this pro football?" Then you realize this *is* pro football, at least back in those days.

We played pretty well, holding the lead for most of the game, up until the fourth quarter. It was a defensive struggle. I had had one pass thrown to me in the whole game, and I was pretty upset. They played a pretty conservative defense, which took away the strong-side receiver, but knowing that didn't make me feel any better. The Vikings put a drive together late, and I think it was Chuck Foreman who scored to give them the fourth-quarter lead, 14-10.

Minnesota had a very smart team, made up of a lot of veterans who had played together year in and year out. They knew what they were doing. They hardly even watched me. When they lined up on defense, they were looking in at the quarterback and would break on the ball. They could still "feel" you split out there, and they were a very difficult defense to throw the ball against.

You didn't get much time to throw because they had those Purple People Eaters like Alan Page, Jim Marshall, and Carl Eller bearing down on the quarterback in no time.

After they scored that late touchdown, we had something like ninety-one yards to go after getting the ball back. The only good thing about that situation was that I knew Roger would be coming to me and asking me what I could get open on. He hit me on a couple of passes to get us up to midfield. On one of those receptions, the one in which I was knocked out of bounds, a security guard came over and kicked me, although I didn't realize it until I saw it on film later because I hadn't felt anything when it happened.

At one point, we got bogged down and found ourselves in a fourth-and-something-like-sixteen-or-eighteen situation. In the huddle Roger said to me, "Why don't you try to run a post corner on Nate Wright and bring it out flat to the sideline? And make sure you get enough for a first down."

One thing about the Vikings is that they did not play a true prevent defense. They played their same defense in that two-minute situation, but just loosened it up a little bit. They played a zone, but if you were in their area, they covered you like they were in a man. I was in Nate Wright's area and he was covering me like mad. So I broke to the post and Nate bit on that, and I knew it was now the time to break it to the corner because Roger is going to be throwing the football under a heavy pass rush.

I look up and the ball is right there, and I caught it going toward the sideline. And Nate hit me. I would have gotten my feet inbounds, but Nate nailed me and knocked me out. I went sliding on the ice and snow on the sideline, and as I went sliding that's when the security guard kicked at me.

Now we're down to about thirty seconds left, and we're out near midfield. Roger called for a swing pass to Preston Pearson coming out of the backfield. Now if Preston had caught the pass, there was a good chance that the Vikings would have pulled him down with the clock running down. We might not have been able to get another play off. But Preston dropped the ball, and that turned out to be a blessing because it stopped the clock.

We get back to the huddle, and Roger's saying, "Hey, we've got to go now. We have to start taking some shots downfield at the end zone." He turned to me and said "Why don't you run a turn-in takeoff?" I had run the same pattern the year before, when Clint Longley had come in to replace Roger in our comeback victory over Washington on Thanksgiving Day, after Roger had gotten knocked out of the game. I ran a turn-in takeoff in the game and Clint had hit me with a touchdown.

Roger said, "Run that same route on Nate Wright. I'll throw it down there and we'll see what happens."

On the snap, I close it in on Nate Wright and then break it in at about twelve yards. Nate bites on that, and so I then take off deep. Nate recovered nicely and we were about even going down the field. As I look back, I could see Roger throwing the ball, but he's underthrowing it. He had already pumped the ball once to fake a pass to Golden Richards running a post pattern. Our main concern wasn't so much Nate Wright as it was Paul Krause, their free safety. We didn't want him coming over the top for a possible interception or to double-cover me. Faking that pass to Golden kept Krause on that other side of the field. By the time Roger had brought his arm back and then thrown it to me, I was well downfield, which is why the ball was underthrown.

I was able to see that, and Nate Wright reacted to me. There was contact on the play, like the kind of jostling you get with two basketball players going up for a rebound. I came back and did what we receivers called "a swim move," in which you take your arm up over the top of the defender to try and get position on the inside. The ball hit my hands as I was doing that, and I thought I had dropped it. But in sliding down, the ball got stuck between my hip and elbow, and I said, "Oh, Lord, I caught the Hail Mary!"

Paul Krause came running over late, and Nate was on the ground. I backed the final five yards into the end zone, and we couldn't believe that we had pulled it off.

Talk about eerie. The stadium had gone from peak exuberance following the Vikings' go-ahead touchdown, and then we score this touchdown against the Purple People Eater defense with just a few seconds left. Their fans are just sitting there stunned. It was a tremendous silence. After I got mobbed by my teammates in the end zone, I had to walk past the Vikings' bench to get to our bench, and those guys were giving me some bad looks. They looked like they wanted to kill me.

NATE WRIGHT:

As I was dropping back, I saw Staubach look over to Golden Richards's side and make a pump. I thought he was throwing that way, but then I saw his eyes come back to Drew. I said, "It's coming this way. I better get on my horse."

I turned and faced up to Drew, and I thought we were running shoulder to shoulder. I saw the ball in the air, and I really thought I could intercept it because I was in good position. Suddenly, my mind became confused. Next thing I knew I was on the ground, and I saw Drew catch the ball on his hip and run into the end zone. I was in shock.[21]

STAUBACH:

I don't think I've ever been in such an eerie stadium. The only noise was our guys whooping and yelling as we headed to our locker room.[22]

STAUBACH *continues:*

Sister Sloan, my first-grade teacher, contacted me. You can't believe the number of nuns and priests who have told me how proud they were that I threw a Hail Mary. Of course, my Baptist friends say I should have called it the Hail Jesus pass.[23]

Back to DREW PEARSON:

The controversy surrounding the play, whether I had pushed Nate Wright or there had been defensive pass interference, keeps the play alive. To this day, people ask me about that play all the time. Of course, Vikings fans to this day are still not over it. Whenever the Cowboys and Vikings play, there will always be Vikings fans with signs that say "Drew Pushed Off."

That was kind of the defining moment in my career, the kind of play that receivers dream about making. I was fortunate enough to make quite a few of them, but none stand out more than that Hail Mary pass.

During his career, Staubach led Dallas to twenty-three comeback victories in his eleven seasons, fourteen of those in the final two minutes or overtime. Of course, there are two ways of looking at that. DAN REEVES:

I used to kid Roger Staubach about pulling games out in the final two minutes. I'd tell him, "That's great, but if you had played better the first fifty-eight, we wouldn't be in that predicament at the end."

But that ability—very few have it. Everybody in the stadium knows you're going to throw, they have set the defense to stop it. You gotta have a tremendous arm and tremendous ability and tremendous poise and tremendous confidence. Staubach had all that. So does John Elway.[24]

DREW PEARSON:

Everyone talks about the Hail Mary game, but the plays that stand out for me, that give me as much if not more pride and satisfaction, was when Roger and I would hit like a third-and-eight pass on a sixteen route, and the whole stadium, as well as the opposing defense and defensive coordinator, would know that the ball was coming to me on a particular route, and we could still execute it and make it work. When we would come back to the huddle and slap each other five, that, to me, was the real feeling of satisfaction.

His leadership was second to none. He could be Mr. Good Guy, Mr. Moral, and all that other stuff, but if he wasn't performing on the field, no one would have been following him. He wasn't just the general on the field; when the ball was snapped, he was making plays, too. Roger did some unbelievable things avoiding sacks, taking hits, running for first downs, drilling the ball in tight situations, reading defenses, and throwing to the right man. He did all of those things very well.

If he hadn't done all these things, you never would have cared that he had played at the Naval Academy, gone to Vietnam, or been a twenty-eight-year-old rookie. He had this kind of magic about him on the field, and it made all these other aspects of life important to people.

With the Cowboys' unprecedented success in the seventies came the inevitable heightened scuttlebutt about money and salaries. The birth of the rival World Football League in 1974, which lured away a number of NFL veterans and draftees, had something to do with that. So did the Cowboy's' notoriously tight purse strings. LEE ROY JORDAN explains:

Roger was making pretty big money in the off-season, so they'd get Roger signed quick, and get him to sign low. After football, after we retired, I told him, "You're the reason no one else could ever get a raise, 'cause they based all the salaries off yours. We had to be X number of percentage points close to you." I told Roger, "You're making $200,000 in the off-season, and I'm making $200. There's a lot of difference in that." He was embarrassed.

But it is true. It's very true. I think that was just like the deal with Tom (Landry) and his salary. They kept that down so they could put up to the players, "Tom is only making $50,000. How could you make more?" I don't know what kind of bonus he'd make, and I know he owned some stock, and that was appreciating very nicely. That was the leverage they had on us, and most of us weren't making enough to split with an agent or an attorney, so we didn't have anybody else involved. And if you brought an attorney, then you *really* got on Tex's bad side.[25]

TEX SCHRAMM *in those days personally handled contract negotiations one-on-one with players, no agents involved:*

I would invite Roger up to the office to talk contract. I would ask him, "What do you want?" He'd say, "I'd be happy with such and such," and I'd say, "You've got a deal." And that was the whole negotiation, and that's the way it went for the rest of his career.

Later in his career, about the time he was getting into the real-estate business and we were having a kind of economic boom around here, he said, "You know, I've made some pretty good investments. What I would like is for the contract to somehow read that as soon as my career is over, some of these obligations I have will be taken care of so that I will never be in debt."

So we made up a contract that would have a good substantial salary while the rest of it was put into a deferral plan that somehow involved loaning him the money on a tax-sheltered basis. We did similar deals with some of our other players in those days, and it worked out well for them.

Roger knew what the salaries were of other players at his position around the league. He said, "I don't think a player should be judged as to what kind of player he is based on the amount of his contract, but solely on his ability." I remember that (Fran) Tarkenton was supposedly making an enormous salary in those days. Roger said, "I know what Tarkenton, (Terry) Bradshaw, and those other fellows are making. I want in some way to be able to cover the investments that I have made."

At that time around Dallas, everyone was buying up all this property. The ones who got into trouble were those that would put some down as a down payment with the idea that they would pay the rest in two or three years, only to not be able to pay down the road. Roger knew about that, and he didn't want to be one of those who couldn't follow through on his investments down the road. He said, "I want to know that if I made an investment that I'm good for that money."

Roger always had a great attitude about accepting responsibility. We never had a contract dispute, and I don't think we ever had a contract negotiation that lasted more than one day. He knew what he wanted, he had figured it out, and he would say, "This is what would be nice to have."

One thing Staubach didn't want was another quarterback controversy, but as 1976 rolled around he soon found himself in a skirmish with third-year reserve Clint Longley, a reportedly self-described rebel who seemed to go out of his way to foster an outlaw image. Two years earlier, Longley had replaced an injured Staubach and, with some bombs-away passing, had led the Cowboys to a dramatic comeback victory over Washington on Thanksgiving Day. Longley saw himself as Staubach's heir apparent, but the feeling wasn't mutual, especially after Danny White came to the Cowboys after two seasons in the WFL. White, who had been drafted in 1974, was the polite, play-it-by-the-rules type of quarterback who meshed well with Landry and

Staubach. When Staubach began to work with White, Longley,
believing he had been wronged, went after Staubach with fire in
his eyes. It was a bad move, as HOLLYWOOD HENDERSON
explains:

Staubach had decided to take Danny White under his wing, to
make the new kid his protégé, the heir to his throne, and that
(angered) Longley. At practice one morning, Clint had let it be
known to Roger in terms that were apparently unacceptable to
Roger's sense of decorum, and Roger had invited him over to the
baseball field to air their differences.

This was a private matter. There wasn't any crowd that gath-
ered to watch, no grandstand and no grandstanding. Just a couple
of Cowboys out to settle a score. It seemed that Roger got the best
of it. Reports from the front said that Roger had picked Clint up
and body-slammed him. You didn't think of Staubach as a fighter;
you'd figure Longley for the one with the fists, but I guess the guy
just didn't like to lose.[26]

DREW PEARSON:

The next day when Clint decided to get revenge on Roger, it was
a beautiful day, another day in paradise in Thousand Oaks. We
were preparing for the afternoon practice, and everything was
going as normal. What was abnormal was finding Clint sitting in
the locker room. The quarterbacks and kickers and punters are
usually the first ones to hit the practice field, so it was unusual for
Clint to be there. . . . He had his pants on, no socks, a little half T-
shirt, and he was sitting there kind of bent over, his foot on the
brace of the chair flicking up and down nervously. . . . I came by
and said, "Clint, you need to get out there." He didn't say anything, didn't respond.·

Roger wasn't there yet, because he had an engagement in
town, but we did not notice that as anything unusual because

since we didn't see him, we thought he was already out on the practice field. When Roger arrived, he was late getting to practice, so he was rushing and hurrying, and he had put on his pants real fast, and he started to put his shoulder pads on, and I didn't see him because I had gone to the back part of the locker room. But I heard the rumbling, the tremendous commotion, and then I ran in to see what was happening.

I saw Roger and Clint really going at it on the concrete floor of the locker room, and there was blood all around, and I found out later the blood was the result of Clint's initial attack on Roger. When Roger got his pads over his head, he couldn't use his arms, and that's when Clint decked him. Roger was caught off-balance and went flying back onto the scale that was there for us to weigh in and weigh out before and after each practice, and he was falling backward, and he turned, and as he turned, his head hit the scale, and blood went gushing everywhere. . . .

Everybody was trying to separate them and nobody could. . . . Roger was still very upset and was really trying to get back at Clint, and once Randy (White) let Clint go, he grabbed his stuff out of his locker and was gone.[27]

More from HOLLYWOOD HENDERSON *on Longley:*

Longley took off. He didn't stick around to try and finish him off like any good street fighter. Didn't wait for Roger to get himself untangled and come after him. Longley wailed through the door in full uniform, shoulder pads and everything, and all of us ran and watched him take off two hundred yards up an embankment toward the dormitories.

Nobody could believe it. Guys fight all the time out on the field, but not quarterbacks, and not in the locker room.

Roger was furious. I'd never seen him like this, never would again. He wanted to kill Clint Longley. He didn't shout or scream; it was worse: he measured the words as he measured the man. . . .

He was biting off the sounds like he was spitting out brimstone. . . . On this day he was a vulgar football player.

Roger bolted to the door trying to take off and get Longley at the dorms, but Jerry Tubbs wouldn't let him. Jerry stood and barred Roger's way until he cooled down some. Roger stood there raging, trying to fight Tubbs to get out the door and go settle this whole deal, but Jerry had handled quarterbacks before and this one didn't get away, either.[28]

JERRY TUBBS *adds his perspective:*

I don't remember exactly what happened, except that Roger was trying to get away to go after him. I think Clint had already run off before I got there, and when I did get there I think it was Randy White who had a-hold of Roger. That's just one more example of Roger being the competitor, and he was never arrogant about that. He didn't care what would happen, he was going to go get Clint.

LARRY COLE:

Clint was kind of a West Texas, free-spirit kind of guy. He had a pistol for shooting snakes. It was nice to see Roger not turn the other cheek, because Longley deserved every bit of that. When we got back to the dorm, a couple of us went in there and got rid of that pistol to make sure that deal didn't go any further. That was the end of the Clint Longley era.

DAN REEVES, *who was still a Cowboys assistant coach at the time, said the net result for Longley probably could have been even worse:*

The Clint Longley thing tells you how competitive Roger was. Roger was livid, being so competitive: He was ready to challenge Clint to a fight in Texas Stadium and sell tickets to it. It was a difficult time and no one could have handled it better than he did. As strong as Roger was from all those workouts and weight work, the only way Clint could ever hit him was from behind. Otherwise, Roger probably would have killed him.

Staubach's last four seasons weren't as eventful off the field, but on the field he solidified his growing reputation as perhaps the best quarterback in the game, at least at the time. He led the Cowboys to the playoffs in each of the last four seasons, including two more Super Bowl appearances (27-10 victory over the Morton-quarterbacked Broncos in Super Bowl XII and a 35-31 loss to the Steelers in Super Bowl XIII). His last season, 1979, was arguably his best in terms of numbers—he passed for more than thirty-five hundred yards and threw twenty-seven touchdown passes against only eleven interceptions. But it was also a season with plenty of headaches that included five Staubach concussions, a three-game losing streak late in the season, and a first-round exit from the playoffs in a 21-19 loss to the Rams. The following March, Staubach, a young thirty-eight, announced his retirement. DREW PEARSON *remembers:*

During the (1979) season Roger had mentioned retirement a few times, because he had so many concussions. He had that severe one against Pittsburgh. But I never thought he would quit, because nobody liked to go out with a loss, and Roger Staubach was like that. We just felt he would be back. It was something he had to deal with during the off-season. He made a calculated decision. . . . I couldn't even go to his press conference, because I didn't want the whole world to see me crying and broken up.[29]

Before finally deciding to retire, STAUBACH *visited medical experts to get the lowdown on his concussions:*

A doctor in New York said the concussions were cumulative and that there was some change in my reflexes from my left to right side. But a doctor in Dallas felt that everything was fine, just that there was some concern there had been so many. Of course, I wanted to be able to make my own (retirement) decision and not have some coach knock on my door. . . . Yet I missed it a heckuva lot more than I realized I would.[30]

TEX SCHRAMM *said he wasn't convinced that Staubach needed to retire, although that might have been rationalized, even wishful, thinking:*

After he had had a few of those concussions, people were telling him, "You oughtta quit. You oughtta quit." The thing that scared him is when he went to a couple of doctors who were not football doctors, and they looked at him and said something like, "You've got so much of your life still ahead of you that you don't need to be risking anything." There's a big difference between doctors who have been in football much of their careers and those that haven't. Those doctors who haven't been around football might not know everything that humans can do. Football doctors can understand what's involved.

Roger was a young thirty-eight when he retired. Remember, there were four years right after college that he didn't play, and those were four years where he wasn't being tackled and getting banged up. And of the times that he got hit hard or received a concussion, none of them were the kind of hits that I would call particularly vicious, like the ones where a guy gets flipped in the air and/or has his head snapped back in a violent hit.

FRANK LUKSA:

He could have played on, no question about it. But he had had a number of concussions. They researched his injury history all the way back to when he was in high school and figured that he had had something like twenty concussions, including a couple of real bad ones—one in Pittsburgh and one in Texas Stadium.

The latter one was the Thanksgiving Day game against the Redskins, before which Diron Talbert of the Redskins had said, "If we can knock out Roger Staubach, we'll have a very good chance of winning." That's what they did, knocking Roger out of the game early, although Clint Longley, the rookie, came in and led the Cowboys to the comeback victory, 24-23, after having trailed 16-3 at one point. I can remember Blaine Nye of the Cowboys saying, in referring to Longley, "It was a victory of the uncluttered mind."

Several years later Roger went to see a couple of neurosurgeons, and there was a difference in opinion as to whether he should continue on. One of them said that Roger was fine, that he could continue on. The other said there was a minute difference of reaction in one of his toes or feet, and he gave Roger a note of caution. Marianne, Roger's wife, said, "Who knows, he may have been born that way." But she was in favor of him hanging it up, as she was getting alarmed about his getting hurt.

When Roger told Coach Landry he was going to retire, Landry told Roger he thought he could still play. Another factor in all this is that Roger was tiring of all the preparation. He was one of those guys who was "first on and first off" when it came to the practice field, in addition to all the off-season work he took it upon himself to do. It got to the point where he felt he couldn't commit himself to that kind of a regimen anymore. That sentiment and the concussions led him to that. He probably could have geared it back a little bit and keep playing, but he didn't believe in giving it just 95 percent. That's the kind of guy he was—he felt if he couldn't devote himself entirely to being fully prepared, he would be cheating not only himself but also the team.

With Staubach retired and Longley long gone, it was Danny White's turn to step out of the apprenticeship and up into the driver's seat. White was good, but he wasn't great, and Landry needed the latter. Landry never again made it to a Super Bowl. With White at quarterback behind a veteran offensive line, several star receivers the likes of Drew Pearson and Tony Hill, and running back Tony Dorsett cranking out thousand-yard seasons, the Cowboys had little trouble putting points on the board. In each of White's first three seasons as starter, the Cowboys made it to the cusp of the Super Bowl, only to lose each time in the NFC Championship game (to the Dick Vermeil-coached Eagles, the Joe Montana-quarterbacked 49ers, and the Joe Gibbs-coached Redskins). After those first three give-him-a-chance seasons, White was having to look over his shoulder at a procession of quarterbacks that Landry threw at White—eventual flameouts such as Gary Hogeboom, Steve Pelluer, and even Kevin Sweeney. Problem was, none of them were named Roger Staubach. Dallas sportscaster DALE HANSEN:

It was almost impossible for Danny White to follow Roger as Cowboys quarterback. I used to do a show on Channel 4 (at the time the Dallas/Fort Worth area's CBS affiliate) with Drew Pearson, and Drew was always complaining about Danny White. And I thought Danny White did some remarkable things. But he was always going to be compared to Roger. And Gary Hogeboom was always going to be compared to Roger. It took about ten years of lackluster football from the Cowboys before people started to accept the fact that Roger doesn't play anymore.

Even when (Troy) Aikman came along, he was being compared to Staubach. At the height of Aikman's success, people would make the argument, "Well, he doesn't bring teams from behind like Staubach did." Of course, that's another one of my favorite jokes, and I like to use it on Staubach. Here he is, famous for bringing his team from behind so many times in the fourth quarter to win. Nobody mentions that on all but one of those occasions he was the quarterback who *put* them behind. Even he laughs at that. Even twenty years from now, in 2022, there will be a segment of the population that will look at whoever the Cowboys quarterback is and say, "Yes, he's very good, but he's no Staubach."

Still, that's how you define *greatness*: by telling me about him ten years after he's gone. Only the great ones *endure*, and there's no question that Staubach has done that.

HANSEN *has been a television sportscaster in Dallas since 1980 and for much of that time has served as radio color man for Dallas Cowboys games. He offers this humorous look back at Staubach:*

The first NFL game I ever saw was Roger Staubach's last game, in 1979. I was working for a TV station in Omaha, Nebraska, and I was in Dallas that weekend because I was covering the Nebraska Cornhuskers in the Cotton Bowl. I got tickets to see the playoff game against the L.A. Rams, which turned out to be his last game, and it gave me a story about Roger that always drives him nuts because I use it to introduce him at every banquet he and I have ever been to.

This is how it goes: I'm sitting in the corner of the end zone having never seen an NFL game in person in my life. Here I am at Texas Stadium with the Dallas Cowboys, Roger Staubach, Drew Pearson, the whole bit. Vince Ferragamo, the former Nebraska quarterback, was playing quarterback for the Rams at the time. So I have some mixed emotions about all this.

With about two minutes to go in the game, Ferragamo throws a touchdown pass to Billy Waddy, and the Rams take the lead.

I'm legitimately thrilled because, one, it's a great game for Ferragamo, and, two, more importantly, I'm going to be there to witness one of the famous Roger Staubach comebacks.

As I tell the story, I've always noticed how Terry Bradshaw went to four Super Bowls and he's got four rings. Roger Staubach has gone to five Super Bowls, and he and Marianne have five kids. I think there's a connection here: Every time Terry Bradshaw goes to a Super Bowl he gets a ring, and every time Roger Staubach goes to a Super Bowl, he and Marianne get a kid.

DALLAS COWBOYS

Staubach with Vice President Spiro Agnew, before Staubach became Captain America and before Agnew unceremoniously became a private citizen again.

So as the game against the Rams played out, I say in my story, Roger drops back to pass on fourth down, and he throws the ball to Herb Scott, the offensive guard. Scott, as Roger will be the first to tell you, makes a helluva shoestring catch. Of course, it's a penalty for throwing to an ineligible receiver, and the Rams go on to finish off winning the game.

Continuing my story, what I then say is that I didn't know, the whole time while I was in the stands yelling for Roger to lead the Cowboys back, was that Marianne was also sitting in the stands, yelling, "Throw the ball to Herb Scott! Throw the ball to Herb Scott!"

Recently, I was at a Father of the Year luncheon and getting ready to introduce Roger yet again, when he looks over at me and tells me, "If you tell that story one more time, I'm going to stop payment on my check to your charity golf tournament." Well, I didn't use the story in my intro as MC, but I went ahead and told it to the people sitting at our table. When I got to the part where I say, "It was fourth down and Roger drops back to pass . . . ," Staubach corrected me—and this is the fascinating thing about great athletes like Staubach—he can tell you the exact down and yard line of about any memorable play. He will tell you that the pass to Herb Scott was on third down, not fourth down.

By the time Staubach retired in 1980, the title "America's Team" was on the lips of almost every fan of pro football in America, either in praise or scorn. GIL BRANDT offers his take on the America's Team appellation:

A part of it is Roger Staubach. Number one, the uniform; without question, our colors (blue, silver, and white) are conducive to feeling good about who's wearing them. How many people want to wear a purple shirt? How many people want to wear a white shirt or a blue shirt?

When you talk about America's Team, there is more involved than just players, even though players and Coach Landry enter into it a great deal. One of the things that Tex did and which Tom reinforced with the players was to answer your mail. You'd walk into the locker room and there would be guys with boxes of shoes and boxes of mail.

It used to gall Tex when he walked in there and saw all these boxes with unanswered mail. He finally instituted a policy where he asked each player to pay the team something like fifty dollars a month and the team would take care of answering all their mail for them. Tex also knew that people would want something like a picture, so we made up all these reproductions of each player's photo and sent them back with a letter, whether it came from

Cedar Rapids, Iowa, or Big Sky, Montana. Consequently, we might not have been the number-one team in Chicago, but we had a lot of fans there and were the number-two team everywhere.

Also, there was Coach Landry and what he stood for. I don't know if anyone really knows how much time he devoted to the FCA (Fellowship of Christian Athletes) and how much money he raised for them. As a result, all of these families saw their sons being able to go to FCA camps in part because of Tom, who furthermore was seen by millions as a man on the sideline who was never acting up, cursing, or doing anything like that. Then there were the players, who for the most part had great character and were also smart players. When we would play in Philadelphia and go into the team hotel there, we had to have guards there because there were so may people there. We'd go to Arizona to play and there would be more people wearing Cowboy jerseys there than there were people wearing Cardinal jerseys.

There was more than just one factor to becoming America's Team. People looked up to Roger Staubach because he had spent four years defending his country. Also, our players were very media savvy. That goes back to answering the mail. Also, most players are thought of as being guys who might get seventeen phone calls and end up returning one. With our guys, everyone who called us got a return phone call, wherever it may be. It's the little things that make it a big thing.

Another thing was having all of our guys wearing ties on road trips. No shirttails hanging out or anything like that, and the guys liked it. What you were doing was also preparing them for life after football—wearing a tie to work five or ten years from now.

TEX SCHRAMM, on "America's Team":

Roger Staubach was the pinnacle of it, because he was the consummate All-American man that you were looking for. Secondly, Tom Landry added a certain amount of class, a foundation to the whole thing. Between those two, if you ever thought you were going to go to war, you wanted to have Tom Landry out there instructing you as to what you were going to do, and you wanted Roger out there executing the plan.

Sportswriter FRANK LUKSA:

I think he was part of it, but he wasn't the entire reason for why the America's Team label came around. A big part of it was NFL Films' noticing how wherever the Cowboys went to play on the road, they always drew a large crowd of fans. That spread the idea of the Cowboys' being America's Team. NFL Films suggested the title to Tex Schramm, and Tex embraced it immediately.

I remember the first time the team saw the film with that title—they were appalled. They knew what was going to happen, that this would be a label that would get thrown back in their faces forever and ever. Staubach said he thought it was a joke at first. You never heard an opposing team say, "We lost to America's Team." But when they beat Dallas, they would crow about beating America's Team.

Staubach fit the image. So did Landry and a lot of the other players. They had universal appeal.

Back to you, DALE HANSEN:

I don't think you would have had America's Team without Roger Staubach. One, you need the navy guy; you need the Heisman Trophy; you need the family guy. That's Roger. You don't have "America's Team" with Don Meredith, even though Meredith was a terrific quarterback. It certainly made it easier having a name like America's Team to sell when you had a guy like Roger Staubach at quarterback. Captain America.

I've said the same thing about Brett Favre, the Packers quarterback: There is something about America that is fascinated by athletes who make it look hard. Staubach, many times, made it look hard, where many times Aikman made it look easy. Aikman made very few mistakes and rarely threw the interception, and it seems like the Cowboys with him at quarterback were almost always ahead in their games. Kareem Abdul-Jabbar—I'm sorry; he made it look too easy. Jack Nicklaus made it look too easy; Arnold Palmer made it look hard. Willie Mays did it gracefully, but he made it look hard, the cap flying off when he made a catch. Then you had Joe DiMaggio, who I don't think ever sweated.

So with the Cowboys you had Tex Schramm, the cheerleaders, Drew Pearson, Calvin Hill, Walt Garrison. . . . Remove Roger Staubach, and you've got a very good football team that is probably a long ways away from being America's Team. Strong religious guy. Clean-cut. Great family man. Always signing autographs. Filling in as a guest speaker at the last minute for a bunch of high school kids, and coming with a prepared speech with all these specific points. *C'mon!!* For many years, I've been thinking there's got to be a chink in that armor, and I've yet to seen it.

The only thing I've heard about him from other guys is that he never made enough money, that he allowed Tex Schramm to, basically, take advantage of him. Roger's take on this has been "Hey, I enjoyed my relationship with the Cowboys and didn't need to make more money." Drew Pearson, say, goes in there and tells Tex Schramm, "I want $250,000," and Tex looks at Drew and says, "Well, Drew, I think you could make a pretty good argument that you're worth $250,000, and so-and-so over at the Eagles"—I think Harold Carmichael of the Eagles was making at least $300,000 at the time—"is making $300,000, and I think you're worth $250,000. But, Drew, we're only paying Roger two and a quarter, and I think we've got to agree that I've got to pay you less than I'm paying Roger." Pearson's like, "That (SOB) Staubach!"

Roger probably was actually one of those athletes who said, "I'm being *paid* to play football?" I think everybody starts out that way when they're about twelve. My question is, What happens to the dream from the time you're twelve until you turn twenty-five? What happens in our society to these guys? Staubach never went there. With him, it was "What are you paying me now? Okay, that's fine." I happen to respect that, guys who live the way we grew up dreaming what it was.

You know, Staubach's Republican and I'm not, but I would vote for him for any office in the country. You don't have to send me any platform information. Send me the ballot, I'll mark it Staubach, and I'm done.

Just for the sake of some balance, let's check in with former defensive tackle MIKE MCCOY, *who spent the seventies playing with the Packers, Raiders, and Giants, much of the while listening to a lot of America's Team talk:*

I thought it was kind of ridiculous, just a marketing ploy, like calling some guys the Four Horsemen and putting them on horses to face pestilence and all that for the sake of a photo.

If anything, the Green Bay Packers with Lombardi, Starr, and those guys had been America's Team. I mean, this was a team that was owned by the people, not by one person or a corporation. In the seventies, you had the Pittsburgh Steelers, which went on to win four Super Bowls. If any team should have been America's team during the seventies, it should have been the Steelers, not only because they won more Super Bowls but also because of what they represented—blue-collar America. They had such a big influence on changing the city of Pittsburgh itself, from this polluted place to a magnificent-looking city.

As for Roger, I think his having served in the navy and spending time in Vietnam added something to the mix in terms of that being America's Team. When you think about it, it's kind of ironic, because Americans for the most part didn't like the Vietnam War at all at that time, and there were many who even looked down on veterans. And Roger was a Vietnam War veteran. There was a real damper on the spirit of patriotism, and here comes this guy who had fulfilled his obligations to the Naval Academy and had gone to Vietnam, and he came back and started his pro career four years after he had last played the game on a high level.

Let's close this chapter with Gil Brandt:

I've had guys tell me all the time now how jealous they were of the Cowboys organization. Two years ago, Dave Wilcox was put into the Pro Football Hall of Fame in Canton. I was up there working for NFL.com, and I hadn't seen Wilcox in something like twelve years. Wilcox was up there addressing the media, and all of a sudden he sees me and says, "There's Gil Brandt—Boy, we used to hate the Cowboys because they got all the publicity. They treated their players better than anybody else, and we always looked forward to playing the Cowboys more than we did anybody else because we wanted to play good enough to destroy their myth."

Teams were fired up to play us every week—we almost always got our opponents' best-played game of the year. I remember Archie Manning running into me once and telling me that he will always remember the first game he ever won as an NFL quarterback (with the New Orleans Saints) because it was against the Dallas Cowboys. That was important to him.

ROGER DA MAN,
IN DEMAND

*F*OR MORE THAN FORTY YEARS, many people, from gasping, grasping defensive linemen to clamoring, adoring fans have been trying to get a piece of Roger Staubach.

Captain America, co-captain of America's Team, quarterbacked his last game nearly a quarter-century ago and to this day has never stepped up to the political plate as long anticipated, or at least as hoped for. Still, he remains a true American icon, a legitimate sports hero and role model whose success has carried from the football field to the business arena. And his involvement with civic and nonprofit organizations is legendary: he belongs to the Fellowship of Christian Athletes, and his civic duties have included serving as national chairman for the American Diabetes Association and national sports chairman and Texas state chairman for Easter Seals.

Staubach began his career in commercial real estate in 1970, working with the Henry S. Miller Company as a vice president

Staubach always has been serious about preparation, even for a friendly round of golf.

during the Cowboys' off-season. In 1977 he and partner Robert Holloway formed the Holloway-Staubach Corporation to conduct brokerage activities. Four years later, in 1981, he went out on his own and founded the Staubach Company, which is involved in commercial land brokerage, corporate and retail services, pension advisory services, and investment and financial services.

Having turned sixty in February 2002, Staubach still serves as president of the company that bears his name. He is still lean and fit, and his lack of pretension when meeting strangers is legendary. He works out a lot and, for real, looks like he could still be playing in the NFL on a limited basis.

JERRY TUBBS:

One thing about Roger is that I can't begin to understand how hard it must be for him to go out in public, especially with his family with him. I can remember one time going to some sort of event with Roger. Driving back late at night we stopped at a gas station. It was after midnight and this was years after Roger had retired. He got out of the car and went into the station to buy something, and he ended up having to autograph a whole bunch of stuff while he was in there. As soon as he walked in the door, the few people there knew who he was and wanted his autograph. All he wanted to do was get a cold drink, and he couldn't even do that.

I can go weeks without people coming up to me, and then every once in a while someone will come up to me, and it makes me feel kind of good. In that respect I wouldn't want to trade places with Roger, even though he always handles it great, and you've got to know that he gets tired of it.

Any veteran sports journalist who doesn't have GIL BRANDT's telephone number in his or her little black book is missing the mark. Brandt's expertise and network of resources have long branched out well beyond football, and yet even he defers to Staubach in the category of people persons:

Roger is a person concerned about other people. What you have now are people who are concerned about themselves and not about the people living next door. Roger was very concerned about his teammates, and I think he walked a very fine line—he understood management's side of things, and yet he understood the football side of things and was able to stay loyal to his teammates. They realized he played when he was hurt; that he worked out when he was hurt. He would come to training camp and run the Landry Mile, even right after he had pulled a hamstring in practice. Here's a guy who would do everything when other people were looking for any reason to get out of it.

No matter how insignificant a person was, Roger always took time to say hello and give a word of encouragement. He's always been the guy who remembers people's names. He's the complete package. There's no question in my mind that if he had run for governor of Texas he would have been elected. He was a unique individual who would have starred at anything he did. He would have been the best sportswriter, and right now he's the best father.

CALVIN HILL *remembers how far Staubach would go to make a new rookie feel at home with the Cowboys:*

As a rookie, you're on your own for the first time. Roger was a married guy, settled down, even as a rookie. When younger players came in, he welcomed them to come to his house and get a home-cooked meal. That's why so many guys bonded with him. He reached out to people.

STAN SHEPPARD, *one of Staubach's good high school buddies who works in the insurance and financial services business, believes he has isolated the key to what has made Staubach so consistently successful:*

If there's any one thing that you could say made him successful, or allowed him to be successful—and I've given a lot of thought to this—it is because he was always prepared when the opportunity to be successful arose. Everybody gets the opportunity to be successful. The problem is, when most people see that opportunity, they try to get themselves in shape only for the opportunity to pass them by.

Why was Roger the quarterback at the Naval Academy? Why was Roger the quarterback with the Dallas Cowboys? Each time, when he got his opportunity, he knew the playbook, he was in shape, and his arm was ready to go. He was ready; he could step in and take over right there, where anyone else would be saying, "Gee, now that I'm getting this opportunity, give me two more weeks to get myself in shape, and I'll be ready to go."

Why is Roger's business successful? Because when the opportunity presents itself, his whole staff is ready to make evaluations, make decisions, and go from there. Life deals you 10 percent; how you handle it is the other 90 percent. That determines the outcome. Roger has always been ready to be successful.

SKIP ORR, *a Naval Academy teammate:*

When you meet him, it's easy to understand why he's been a successful businessman. He would be successful at anything he tries. He is so disarming, for one thing. When people meet him for the first time, they are always struck by how down-to-earth he is. Anybody, and I mean anybody, who sits down with him can see him as a guy "who will connect with me and is attentive to what I have to say." He really does a good job of putting people at ease.

How he handled his fame is a story unto itself. When he started to be in the public eye, it's almost like in his mind that it was sort of expected and it wasn't a big deal, where for everybody else it was. It just didn't affect anything he did. This had something to do with having a great grasp of his own skills, a strong self-awareness, along with the confidence that he had and the fact that he didn't like to lose. It was almost expected in his own mind, even when he went to the Cowboys. All this admiration? That just goes with the territory, and it's no big deal for him.

VINCE EYSOLDT, *another former Purcell classmate, says all the attention on Staubach has come with a price—a loss of privacy and a high level of self-awareness:*

He is so protective of what he does in public because he doesn't want things to be construed the wrong way. That's why he likes getting together with his friends down at his summer home at

PHOTO COURTESY OF ROGER STAUBACH

Roger and Marianne, sweethearts since grade school.

Horseshoe Bay near Austin, Texas. He can be himself. He doesn't have to worry about someone looking over his shoulder when he's laughing at something really funny but someone else will take the wrong way.

One day he was at church and there came a part in the service when people held up their right arm to bless this or that, and he was fearful of raising his right hand because someone might see this and think he's doing the Nazi Hitler salute. To live under that kind of spyglass has to be horrendous. At Horseshoe Bay he's a lot more relaxed and freer, just like in the olden days. He'll pull pranks, too, where in real life he doesn't have a chance to pull real pranks.

Much of Staubach's humor will never be seen in public, for obvious reasons of protective discretion. GIL BRANDT shares a story of Staubach's daring sense of humor:

One of the funniest things I ever saw Roger do was the time he surprised Tex. Tex had this habit of, while talking on the telephone in his office, to swing his chair around and look up the expressway from his office window eleven stories up. There was a ledge outside Tex's window that was about three feet thick, and all of a sudden there's Roger on the outside knocking on Tex's window. Roger had talked the building engineer into letting him get outside on the ledge. Yeah, Tex was rattled.

Veteran sportswriter FRANK LUKSA *vouches for Staubach's humor:*

Roger was always accessible. He was a standup guy after the game, win or lose. A lot of people don't realize that he had a terrific sense of humor. That's not to say he was a clown. I remember one time when they had a game well in hand at Texas Stadium. There was a time-out, and Roger came over to the sideline to get the next play. Landry is standing there and looking up at the hole in the roof, and Roger is just standing idly by, tapping his foot, waiting for Landry to say something. Later Roger said, "I always wondered where he got his plays from."

Staubach also had a terrible disfigured little right finger. It had been dislocated and broken, and it had calcium deposits and was crooked. It was just an awful thing to look at. Someone finally asked him one time, "Why don't you get that finger fixed?" He said, "I don't want to do that. This gets me in handicapped parking."

WALT GARRISON:

I like to pick on Roger because he's such a good guy and he can take it. But he can also dish it out. That's another thing about him. People don't realize how funny Roger is. He is a *funny* guy. Even Coach Landry had a sense of humor, but no one ever saw it. People used to ask me if I had ever seen Coach Landry smile, and I'd say, "No, but I only played nine years. But I know he must have smiled at least three times in his life because he has three kids."

Roger gets compared a lot to Coach Landry because they're both good Christian men, have been married to the same wife forever, and are pretty stoic. But Roger has a great sense of humor.

There were some things that Coach Landry and Roger didn't agree on, especially who was to do the play calling.

Former public-relations maestro L. BUDD THALMAN *happened to work with both of the first two Heisman Trophy winners to go on to also make it into the Pro Football Hall of Fame:*

A good moment for me was when Roger was inducted into the Pro Football Hall of Fame. I went to the induction ceremony because O. J. (Simpson) went in on the same day, and I had been public relations director for the Buffalo Bills for part of the time that O. J. was there. In his remarks, Roger said something like, "There are so many people to thank that I can't thank all of them individually. They know how important they have been in my life." Then O. J. gets up there, and he goes out of his way to thank me for everything I had done for him. When it was all over, Roger came up to me and said, "You're probably mad at me."

One of the things I got a kick out of was when Roger and O. J. were talking about being the first two Heisman Trophy winners elected to the Pro Football Hall of Fame, and O. J. said to Roger, "You've got to remember, Roger, that I am actually first in because 'Si' comes before 'St,' so alphabetically I'm the first Heisman winner in the Pro Football Hall of Fame."

THALMAN *also found it humorous just how detail-oriented Staubach could be:*

Roger has never forgiven me for having his picture taken (for file photos) during his Navy days without the facemask on his helmet. In those days, we took pictures without facemasks on the helmet so you could see the guy's face. All the photographs of him from that time show him without a facemask, even though it was only a single bar then. He said, "That's the phoniest-looking picture. It's not real! I hate that picture!"

Almost forty years after graduating from Annapolis, and even having never achieved the rank of admiral, Staubach still gets the VIP treatment when he shows up at the Naval Academy gates every now and then.
Former Navy assistant coach STEVE BELICHECK *explains:*

Staubach, Navy quarterback, in a pose, sans the faceguard on the helmet.

Tom (Lynch) was probably the best football captain at Navy in all the years that I was there. He went on to become an admiral and then the superintendent of the academy. They had a reunion of players from that era after spring practice this past year (2002). Lynch was telling me that he and Roger drove over together. Tom was driving, and when they got to the main gate, Tom told the security guard, "I've got a letter from the superintendent saying that I was a former superintendent and a retired navy admiral, and here's also my navy ID and retirement papers." The guard studies Tom's stuff and then gives it back to him before looking over at Roger in the passenger side and saying, "Sir, may I see your ID?" Roger hands the guard his billfold, and the guy looks at Roger's ID and says, "Holy sh—! You're Roger Staubach, the greatest football player who ever lived?!" He gets on the phone to call his superiors and says, "You won't g—d— believe who I've got out here!!" Tom later said, "Jeez, I made no impression at all on this fellow, but Roger . . ."

MIKE MCCOY, *the longtime NFL defensive lineman who*
played against Staubach and the Cowboys about a half-dozen
times, got to know Staubach better off the field than on. For
one thing, he was easier to catch. For another, they are both
active in being disciples for their faith:

I got to know Roger fairly well, not from playing against him on
the field but for some of the things we were involved with off the
field. Back in 1971 I joined Bill Glass Ministries—Bill was a former player with the Cleveland Browns—and Bill had felt chal-
lenged to start going into prisons to minister to prisoners. No one
else had been doing that.

Bill prayed about it, and he started by going into a jail in
Merion, Ohio. He said he wanted to get some people from various
local churches to join him because he wanted people from different religious backgrounds. He said he would also get some athletes to go with him to get these guys out of their cells and onto
the rec yard to make themselves available. That first group
included Tom Landry and Roger Staubach, as well as a couple of
other guys.

After we had gotten out into the prison yard, Roger started
throwing a football around, and some of the guys starting taunting him with things like," "Aw, c'mon, can't you throw any harder
than that?" One guy was a former high school wide receiver. He
went out for a pass and Roger zipped one into him and broke the
guy's little finger. That broke the ice, and Roger was able to share
his faith with the prisoners.

Roger came in a few other times as well. I wasn't with him this
one particular time, when Roger went to visit this big prison down
in Florida in the mid-seventies. There was a guy in the crowd that
day by the name of Jack Murphy, who was serving a life sentence.
Jack was a big Dallas Cowboys fan and he went out to hear Roger
speak. Jack ended up receiving Jesus Christ as his personal Savior
out on that field, and it literally changed his life. Jack is out now
and on staff with Bill Glass, and he's dynamite as a prison
speaker—in large part because of Roger Staubach.

Adds McCoy:

Roger does a lot of things off the field that people don't know about. I was involved with him in a conference called Pro Athletes Outreach, started by Athletes in Action in the early seventies. It was a conference for professional athletes and their families during the off-season to come and learn about God's Word in areas such as marriage and finances. Roger came several times to that conference, which added a lot to the whole thing. He didn't have to come. It was a conference for people of all different faiths, so there was Roger, a Catholic, working alongside others of Protestant faiths. He could relate to anybody.

Staubach was in CALVIN HILL's *wedding, and their friendship dates back to when they were both rookies with the Cowboys in 1969. Hill:*

I was in divinity school when I first went to the Cowboys. A lot of the players would go to Orlando's, a pizza place, on Wednesday nights. It wasn't a bad place, but it was a place where the various temptations were there, such as beer, fans, and, I imagine, groupies. It was off-limits to rookies, although Roger was given a "pass" to go there because even though he was a rookie, he really wasn't "a "rookie" because he had already been to training camp before.

Roger and I would go to movies together on Wednesday nights to a theater within walking distance. One time I asked him why he didn't go to Orlando's, and he said he felt it wasn't a place where a married guy should go. I said to him, "Well, being that you're married, you should also be strong enough to see yourself through those temptations." That's when he reminded me, "You know, the spirit is willing, but the flesh is weak." That's from the Bible. The idea is to not put yourself in a testing situation, because then it becomes easy to rationalize things. "I could probably rationalize not telling my wife if I went there, but I couldn't keep it from God."

Roger is what he is. He's the genuine article. We have disagreed on many things, such as politics, but he sticks to his convictions.

Purcell High School classmate JERRY MOMPER *talks about Staubach's continued ties to his longtime friends:*

With all of the success he has had, he could very easily have forgotten all about Cincinnati, Ohio, and all his friends from there. With his parents deceased, he doesn't have a lot to bring him back here now. All the rest of us have pretty much stayed in Cincinnati. It's amazing how he has gone to the trouble to stay so much in touch with so many of us, which is another thing that shows you what kind of guy he is.

My take, from knowing some of the Naval Academy guys who also work for the Staubach Company, is that he's this way with his friends from Annapolis as well, and to some degree his old teammates from the Cowboys.

BOB GRAMANN, *also a fellow Purcell alum:*

That's unusual. I keep in touch with a lot of guys, but I still live here. Roger always valued not only the tradition and what the institution of Purcell stands for, but he also valued the friendships. When you shake it all out in this life, it's all about your family, friends, and your health.

I think Roger always kept his priorities pretty damn straight, not just Purcell but also in everything since, including his business life. And that's God, family, and then your business. Keeping those priorities straight allowed him to be very successful

Staubach and son Jeff playing toss with the football.

and earn the respect of a lot of people. He wasn't just a jock; he was involved in other organizations.

He wasn't one of the wild guys, that's for sure. He kept his nose out of trouble. He wasn't interested in overindulging or getting into a scrap.

PAT DONNELLY *recalls a recent reunion of Naval Academy classmates that brought out Staubach's finely tuned competitive juices:*

The academy superintendent and Roger had been talking before the reunion about putting together a pickup basketball game. The superintendent recruited some of his classmates who were in the area, such as his twin brother, who was an admiral in Washington, D.C., and another admiral who was commander in chief of the Atlantic Fleet. A lot of rank was on that team, where our team was all former football players no longer on active duty in the navy.

This was at a time when Roger had been asked to consider a nomination to be Secretary of the Navy. We were playing best out of three in games to ten, with baskets counting as one point. Each team won one, and then we lost the third game. Roger was kind of upset because he felt these other guys were taking advantage of some questionable calls and noncalls. So half in jest, he told the superintendent and two other admirals, "I might soon be Secretary of the Navy, and if I am, I'll be demoting all of you." He was only kidding, but he was upset about losing.

JERRY TUBBS *weighs in with a view of Staubach's continued ties with former Cowboys teammates:*

I wouldn't say I'm one of his best friends, but I am a friend. Let's just say I don't go over and play basketball with him, but we do get together occasionally with the (Lee Roy) Jordans, the (Chuck) Howleys, the (Tony) Liscios, and some others. The wives are the ones who really initiate a lot of this stuff. For about fifteen years we've been having social functions together. If someone's daughter is getting married, they will give her a shower. If someone has a baby, we'll give a present, and if someone's child is getting married we'll get together for the wedding. Between all the weddings, birthdays, and babies being born, we get together quite often. There's always something.

DON MEREDITH *retired from the Cowboys and the NFL on July 10, 1969, which just happened to be the day Staubach completed his four-year commitment to the navy:*

There's not anyone I have more admiration and respect for than Roger Staubach. I was very impressed with how he took time off from the navy to come to training camp with the Cowboys. I knew right then I had somebody who wanted my job pretty badly.

The thing about Roger is that he is a giver, not a taker. I wish I could have had the chance to spend more time with him over the years so I could have gotten to know him better.

CALVIN HILL *once leaned on Roger for some assistance in picking a name for his baby boy, who would grow up to be a basketball star at Duke and in the National Basketball Association:*

PHOTO COURTESY OF ROGER STAUBACH

Jeffrey Grimes gets a lift from a pickup-hoops-lovin' grandpa.

When my son was born, I had all these girl's names ready for the baby, but not a boy's name. I didn't want to set myself up with a bunch of boy's names and then have a girl who might then spend the rest of her life thinking, *I'm the boy my father never had.* So I picked a bunch of girl's names so I could be all excited when it was a girl. When it was a boy, all of a sudden I had no boy's names.

When he was born, I was euphoric and too busy touching and feeling and reveling in his birth to think about a name. So Grant actually went unnamed for two days. I dragged Roger over to the hospital after a short Saturday practice. When he got there and saw our baby boy, the first thing Roger asked was, "Well, what's his name?" "I haven't thought about it yet," I said. And Roger said, "Hey, he's two days old; he can't go through life as Baby Boy Hill."

When he started talking to Janet, my wife, he brought it up again. So we all sat there for about ten minutes thinking about names, and finally we named him Grant Henry Hill. My father's first name was Henry, and Grant is my mother's maiden name. Roger was pushing it, helping us think it through. My wife liked the name Grant, and Roger said he liked it, too.

Sportswriter SKIP BAYLESS *covered the Dallas Cowboys for many years as an insightful Dallas newspaper sports columnist with a keen eye:*

I mentioned in a column that I'd seen Staubach, crowned by *Sports Illustrated* the week before as "the NFL's Sir Gallahad," drinking a beer on a charter flight home. (Staubach) told me he was torn between having to live up to his image as God's Quarterback and having to answer sackfuls of say-it-ain't-so mail from Bible Belters. How many other NFL quarterbacks had to hire a secretary (Roz Cole) just to answer mail? I received thirty or forty letters myself, mostly from mothers saying I'd ruined their children by printing trash about Roger Staubach's drinking. I'd all but said there was no Santa Claus. "You're really going to love Dallas," Staubach kept telling me.[1]

Cowboys linebacker LEE ROY JORDAN *spent a number of years as Staubach's roommate on the road and at training camp:*

I had also roomed a few years with Don Meredith, so I was privy to a real contrast there. It was a lot more dull having Roger for a roommate.

Roger and I were both real strict about following rules such as curfew. In fact, I think that's why Coach Landry had me room with Don—so that I could help get him in before curfew all the time. Roger and I were always there early. We both wanted to lead by example. Most of the time we were studying game films or studying the playbook the night before a game. We'd go to a team meeting, go to dinner, then go back to our room to watch some TV and go over the game plan one more time. That was our customary routine.

WALT GARRISON:

That time he dipped snuff in trying to be one of the guys, he got sick as a dog. His hair started sweating.

DAN REEVES *had this to add in attesting to Staubach's competitiveness:*

We used to run a mile and a half after working on weights each Monday. I don't care, somebody could start two minutes ahead of Roger—we had kind of a cross-country route that we ran across the big field—he was always the first one back. He was not going to let somebody beat him running.[2]

Next up, HOLLYWOOD HENDERSON, *who had this to say about a Super Teams Superstars competition in Hawaii that included Staubach but not him. Regardless, Henderson flew out there on his own and checked into the same hotel:*

Roger was practicing for the swimming event when I met him by the pool. "Hey, Roger," I called to him, "you want to race?" I didn't have any swimming trunks, so I just stripped down to my bikini briefs and dipped my feet in the water.

Roger, an old navy man, looked over to me. He'd graduated from the Naval Academy and had spent (four) years in the service before he had returned to play ball, so I figured he was the man to beat.

Roger is a fierce competitor. All of a sudden he transformed from this nice, happy-go-lucky guy into this maniac who was going to turn into a motorboat. The smile just washed from his face.

We hit the water, him with a racing dive, me with what I learned at the public pools. I beat him by one body length.[3]

JERRY TUBBS *holds Staubach in high regard as a money man, as president of the Staubach Company:*

That's a pretty big responsibility and he's got a lot of people depending on him. You can't believe how they participate in all these charities. Roger never says anything about how they contribute money, but I will read in the paper, it seems like every week or two, how the Staubach Company gave $20,000; Staubach Company, $10,000; Staubach Company, $50,000. God! I told Roger one time at a party, "Do you think you could start a charity for me?" He said, "I don't think that'll work."

Many of Staubach's former teammates have gone to work for him, including SKIP ORR, *who spent nearly twenty years as a pilot for Eastern Airlines and is now a vice president working out of the Staubach Company's offices in northern Virginia, right outside Washington, D.C.:*

He took a chance on bringing me into the company when I had no experience in this particular industry. But Roger is very good, I think, at analyzing people and what their skills might be. He's not the kind of guy who would bring somebody in just to do them a favor.

He started talking to me about two years before I ended up coming here because I was still working for Eastern Airlines as a

pilot. He knew things
were headed downhill
at Eastern, and he
would say, "Gee, if
that doesn't work out,
then at least come and
take a look at the
company." So I went
to Dallas one time,
while I was still work-
ing for Eastern, just to
get a feel for what the
company did. I was
very busy for Eastern
not only flying but
also working as a
national spokesper-
son for the pilots

PHOTO COURTESY OF ROGER STAUBACH

*Staubach helps granddaughter Jordan Gates
celebrate her birthday.*

union and giving speeches to different groups. It's not like I had a
lot of time to plan for what I was going to do after all this time
with Eastern came to an end.

I'm now a senior vice president with the Staubach Company,
managing the consulting group here and am one of the ten part-
ners in the federal practice group. I can't go through a day when
my relationship with Roger doesn't come up somehow. I don't
bring it up, but it's always right there. Just the name of the company carries with it a reputation for integrity and professional-
ism. People will say, "Staubach—isn't that the football player?"
And I'll say, "Yeah." It's a great marketing tool to have the image
of what Roger stands for to be the image of the company you
work for.

Former Cowboys general manager TEX SCHRAMM *continues to
be surprised by Staubach's varied exploits:*

You didn't think of Roger as an intellectual, but then you see him turn around and have tremendous success in one of the toughest businesses there is. It was a different kind of smart. It gets back to being able to make the right decisions and do the right thing.

If he had gotten into politics and run for office, there's no telling how far or how high he could have gone. I keep asking him about it. I always thought his first ambition would be to be governor (of Texas). He could have been elected to about anything he chose to be. I don't think he's ever going to run now.

W. STEPHEN MEEK, *one of Staubach's brokers in the early eighties:*

Other real estate firms are boiler rooms where you're pressured to produce. I work my butt off for the guy because he doesn't stand over me with a whip. We're the exception in our high-pressured profession.[4]

ROBERT EDGE, *an office broker with a competing commercial real-estate firm in the Dallas area:*

He is an incredibly tough competitor, and that carries into the real estate world. He has become our toughest competitor on a day-to-day basis in Dallas. We have taken some assignments that he would like to have, and he has won some that we would like to have. They haven't done anything different, but they've sold it better. He's had a lot of energy and energetic people, and they've created an image of having something revolutionary. And they've done a pretty good job of performing.[5]

BILL LAWLEY, *president of a Dallas realty company:*

It's like competing with a movie star. The difference is, I go into a customer's office and make a presentation, and I say, "I hope the chairman liked me." Roger goes in, and the chairman says, "I hope Roger liked me."[6]

ROZ COLE, *Staubach's longtime public relations coordinator, started working for Staubach in 1972, when he was a fourth-year Cowboys player needing a lot of help in answering his steady onslaught of mail:*

He's worked hard to establish himself as a business person and not just a personality who is a figurehead. A lot of people think he just has his name on the company and doesn't put in much time. But he's personally involved in all facets of it. He studied real estate and got his license while he was still a player. It's something he's always had an interest in and something he works hard at.[7]

CLIFF HARRIS, *former Cowboys teammate and fellow businessman:*

Whether it's sports or business or whatever, I think he enjoys being put in a position where he has to perform. That's where you see Roger come alive and do what he does best, and that is perform under pressure.[8]

CALVIN HILL *would be surprised, but not shocked, to see Staubach at sixty to come out of retirement and give it another go at football. Consider hockey's Gordie Howe, and let's not forget George Blanda, who was fiftyish when he finally*

retired from pro ball and was not in the kind of shape that
Staubach is today:

Roger is sixty now, and I've seen him throw. He could probably play a game or two now, especially with all these rules they now have to protect the quarterback. His style of play as a scrambler and strong dropback passer would have made him a good fit for almost any type of offense over the last twenty years or so.

Egg Staubach on enough, and he'll show you how hard he can
throw a football, as SPORT *magazine once reported:*

A few kids were idly tossing a football around with Roger Staubach in the downtown Cincinnati Club. Staubach was home on brief Christmas leave from the Naval Academy. Suddenly, from across the room, a fellow in his twenties yelled, "So, this is the great Roger Staubach, huh?" Calmly, Staubach gripped the ball twice and threw it easily to the heckler. Each time the fellow returned it—along with more verbal abuse. Finally, Staubach took dead aim and fired hard. As the ball made its violent impact, the heckler's watch flew off his wrist and crashed against a wall. The bewildered fellow walked off, staring at the pieces in his hand.[9]

Veteran Dallas television sports anchor DALE HANSEN:

I've been in this business about twenty-five years, and I've had many great opportunities to meet a lot of great superstar athletes. At the same time, I've had lots of chances to meet some tremendous human beings. But, unfortunately, they rarely are one and the same. One of the rare exceptions is Roger Staubach, who is to me, and always has been, the single best superstar athlete/human being I've ever met in my life.

To this day he still dominates Texas and is one of the most gifted guys in all aspects. As hokey as it sounds, I love the guy. Here it is almost twenty-five years after he's retired, and I can still clearly remember when he was playing for Navy and then the Cowboys. He simply embodies so many things that we grew up believing our great athletes were. He was one of the few who actually pulls it off.

Being Staubach's favorite receiver while with the Cowboys didn't curry DREW PEARSON any favors when they squared off in various "friendly" games:

Many times on Saturday morning I would be over at his house playing basketball with him and other guys. He loves basketball and loves to compete at that as well. One thing about him is that he likes to shoot the basketball. Pass him the ball, and you won't get it back. Yeah, you could call him a gunner, but it's okay because he makes a lot of them.

One of my favorite stories about his competitiveness was the time we both took part in a local superstars competition with some other well-known athletes in the area. This was sometime in the late seventies. There was this one guy, Brian Duncan, who had gone to SMU and was now playing fullback for the Cleveland Browns. One of the events was the football throw for distance. Roger steps up there and throws the ball about sixty yards. Then this Brian Duncan gets up there and throws it about sixty-five yards.

After I see this, I go over to Roger and say, "Don't worry. I'm not going to let you lose to no fullback." So it comes my turn and I end up throwing it seventy-two yards and beat both of them. I kept my promise: No way was I going to let Roger lose a passing contest won by a fullback. I had an arm back then, even though I didn't look very pretty doing it.

Roger and Marianne Staubach and their entire brood.

CALVIN HILL *likewise has seen the side of Staubach that loves basketball:*

When Grant was a junior at Duke, Jeff (Staubach) came down with Roger when Roger was invited to speak at a youth day at Duke in conjunction with a football game. He spoke that morning before the game. After the football game, the Duke basketball team had its first public scrimmage, what they call the Blue-White Scrimmage. It's a big event, considering the popularity of basketball at Duke.

On our way over to see the Blue-White Scrimmage, Roger said, "You know, I'd like to get a workout in before the scrimmage." I said, "Let me take you over and introduce you to Coach K (Duke basketball coach Mike Krzyzewski, and I'm sure they'll let you use their gymnasium." They established a bond real quickly, because of their backgrounds, with Coach K having gone to West Point. I asked Coach K if they had a place where Roger could work out. He said, "Sure." They had a couple of Stairmasters and other machines in the coaches' locker room, and Roger went and worked out.

After that, Coach K went to Roger and said, "Before the game, we have an alumni scrimmage in which players from our past varsity teams come back and play a one-quarter scrimmage.

Would you like to play?" You had guys who had recently graduated to guys dating back to the 1938 team, so you had some guys
seventy or eighty years old out there. Roger said, "Sure, I'd love to
play, but I'm not an alumnus." Coach K said, "Don't worry about
it, we'll make you an honorary alumnus."

Roger dressed out, they introduced him, and he got a big
hand. When he got into the game, he made his first three-point
shot. I was sitting with Jeff in front of some other students, and I
overheard one student say to another one, "I can't believe that's
Roger Staubach. He hasn't played basketball in probably twenty-
five years." And Jeff said, "Yeah, yeah, he played for only three
hours yesterday."

Roger had fun playing in the game, and there were even guys
playing from his era, like Jack Marin. Jeff ended up going to Duke
and playing varsity baseball.

WAYNE HARDIN, *Staubach's football coach at Navy:*

The worst thing you could probably say about Roger is that he
liked double-dipped ice-cream cones.

FRANK LUKSA, *got to know Staubach even better after the
latter retired, when they worked on a book together in 1980:*

He asked me to do it with him. I'd go over to his house with a tape
recorder, and we'd sit down and start talking. All I know is that it
was a hurry-up project: I wrote the entire thing in eighty-nine
days on a manual typewriter. I took a leave of absence from my
newspaper job to do it.

There were a lot of things that he would not talk about, such
as how much money he had given people over the years and what
other kinds of favors he had done for people. I already knew of

many instances in which he had loaned money to people, sometimes when there was no prospect of his ever getting the money back. He revealed a lot about his football career, but not much about his personal life.

The thing about Roger is that he scrambles when he talks. He'd start talking about something, and then end up with an incomplete sentence or thought before jumping over to something else. What you have to do with him is somehow interpret what he's saying or get him to come back to something to complete the thought.

We'd do at least an hour at a time; it all depended on his schedule. It was interesting to me because it made *The New York Times* best-seller list. I told him that if he had had a better career, we could have sold more books. One thing about the book was that Roger would not do much to personally promote it. He made only one or two appearances, because he didn't like to capitalize on his celebrity. "It was embarrassing," he said, referring to the fact that it really wasn't in his nature.

VINCE EYSOLDT, *high school buddy and lifelong friend:*

You're fortunate to have a friend like that to grow up with, and sometimes you don't appreciate it until it's all over. Even today, I bounce some things off him to see how he would handle certain things in life, not necessarily business-related.

ROGER SPEAKS OUT

*R*OGER STAUBACH HAS NEVER hosted *Saturday Night Live*, written a scathing tell-all version of his memoirs, or played *Hardball* with Chris Matthews. That's not his style. On the other hand, Staubach has almost always been willing to answer any question that begs an opinion, a self-examination, or an explanation for why the Redskins were again able to shut down the passing lanes. In his playing days he was readily accessible for media grilling in the locker room. Even today he operates remarkably free from layers of corporate PR flak when inquiring minds come calling.

Staubach never has churned out dozens of pithy and memorable quotes in the manner of a Vince Lombardi or a Bear Bryant. Yet his opinions, statements, and answers to questions have occasionally offered insights of a sort above and beyond the usual jockspeak. A few dozen of his more memorable observations are offered here.

On his newsworthiness:

After you get by the late NFL start because of my navy career and Vietnam, I'm not very interesting on a day-to-day basis.[1]

On his image:

Stories often mention that I don't smoke, drink, curse, or run around. Three out of four isn't bad. I've never said I don't drink. I enjoy having a beer or two after a game. I also drink wine occasionally. I just don't advocate using alcohol.[2]

I've never strived to have an image. I want to be what I am, not what a reporter sees me as being.[3]

On leadership:

Even if you don't believe down deep that things are going to work out, you don't let the other guys know that. You have to fake it sometimes.[4]

On his faith:

When you look at the master plan that Jesus gave to us when He died on the cross on Friday and rose from the dead on Sunday so our sins could be forgiven, now we're talking about something permanent, eternal. We're temporal beings. It is all going to end for us. But He gave us permanence. If you keep that in perspective, you can pretty well handle the ups and downs of this life. That is true in athletics. I was probably able to handle the losses better because I knew there were other things in life that had greater meaning than that particular event.[5]

My faith, my Christianity, keeps me from being a complacent player because I know that there is something much greater than what we are here for in the Super Bowl.[6]

I don't know why people are afraid to talk about God today. You mention God and it's (considered) ridiculous. They put a halo on you or call you a fanatic. That's not right.[7]

Life would be insignificant without a relationship to God.[8]

I am proud to be a Catholic and proud of the stands my Church has taken on such matters as racism and abortion. But, somehow, the Church is missing opportunities to get the message of Christ and spiritual values across to young people today.[9]

I practice my faith. I believe in witnessing, but I believe in doing it more through example than by talking about it.[10]

I believe in Christian principles, being faithful to my wife and caring about people. If that's "square," that's my life.[11]

I do know this: I believe in Jesus Christ as the son of God. . . . He is my Lord, and I believe He loves all with a constant and intense love. I believe in the Bible as His Word, but I am very concerned when fellow Christians start using it so strictly, allowing little interpretation to judge the worthiness and the chance of salvation of all other people. It disturbs me when the fundamentalist Christian says the Jewish person is not saved because of ignoring Christ. I believe that all people have a chance for salvation, based on their own situation and God's all-fair judgment. . . . I can't see how drinking, eating, dancing, and enjoying the things of this earth can be wrong. So many people make religion seem like a "shall not" religion. I believe religion is a "do" religion, a religion of love, so I welcome the disappearance of the overoccupation with sin and the greater accent on loving, caring, and doing for others.[12]

On the perception of football as a violent sport:

If I thought football was a violent game, I wouldn't be playing it. I'm just a skinny little guy trying to use my talents out there on the field.[13]

On morality:

I'm very concerned about public morality and leadership, but I'm sure not going to set myself up as an authority.[14]

On his frustration in 1971 while sharing Cowboys quarterbacking duties with Craig Morton:

I have to play more than a half, more than a game or two to get things going. If Coach Landry doesn't want to take a chance with me, someone else will. If things don't work out here, I think there's someone who'll throw me out there and say, "Hey, win for us."[15]

On his picking the Naval Academy over other better-known schools:

I don't want to goof off. I need to go to a school that will teach me some discipline.[16]

Joking about his scrambling:

Coach Landry wasn't happy with my scrambling. It caused a running feud between us. But I put up with his play calling, and he put up with my scrambling.[17]

On his speech during his induction into the Pro Football Hall of Fame:

The only things I forgot were God and my parents.[18]

On the world of business:

Business has its cycles. It has its periods of time when things are going well and you get complacent, and all of a sudden, you've got to rethink and restructure how you do things. You have to be a little bit paranoid about where your business is even when it's successful.[19]

On meeting challenges on and off the football field:

In real estate, there are just as many challenges as football. And the similarity with sports is that good things don't happen unless you work toward making them happen.[20]

I've always been fairly determined in business, but as an athlete I was *not* the same person. I can compete in perseverance and intensity with anybody. Off the field I'm a family man—more even keel.

But in the athletic environment you just have to realize these guys are out there to hurt you and take something from you.[21]

Responding to TV sportscaster Phyllis George's on-air question about whether he compared himself to sexually active bachelor quarterback "Broadway Joe" Namath:

I enjoy sex as much as Namath, but only with one woman.[22]

On being in the public eye:

Being in the public eye is no license to suggest how people should live or govern themselves. Renown alone is hardly a credential.[23]

On his winning the Heisman Trophy in 1963:

Near the end of the year the press said I would win the Heisman Trophy, but to me it was, "What kind of deal is that?" The ramifications were no way like they are today.[24]

On his injury-plagued senior season at Navy:

I only had about four or five games that were effective. After I won the Heisman Trophy as a junior, it was a big disappointment. And I thought it was the end of my football career.[25]

His response as a Midshipman while riding an elevator that opened to a woman asking him if it was going up or down:

No, ma'am, it's going to the right.[26] (The unsuspecting woman thanked him and didn't get on.)

On the game of football:

Isn't it funny how football can become such a big thing? Think of it—just a game.[27]

On his uncanny ability to avoid pass rushers:

My reactions are pretty fast, and I have good peripheral vision. Sometimes when I get back there and drop to pass, I know someone's going to get me, so I guess I just duck at the right time.[28]

On uncertainty:

I've learned in psychology that you're supposed to shoot for the top. Down deep I think I can, but I don't want to be disappointed if I don't make it.[29]

On his alleged color blindness:

I'll bet I've taken more eyes tests than any man in America. Guys will come up to me and say, "Hey, Rog, what color is that chair?"[30]

On serving some of his service time at sea, far away from Marianne:

I never really cared for sea duty—the long separations.[31]

On Craig Morton, his quarterback rival during his first five-plus seasons with the Cowboys:

We have always been good friends off the field, and I've always wished him well. And that's no sea story.[32]

On being in shape:

Being in shape gives me confidence. Quarterbacks have to be confident.[33]

On mental toughness:

Mental toughness is the one thing all top quarterbacks share, regardless of how they conduct their lives off the field. That and concentration.[34]

On the dangers of serving in Vietnam as a supply officer:

Mainly the things you worried about were terrorist-type things— they'd put a hand grenade in the officers' club or something. But I wasn't in one of those precarious jobs like the guys who were classmates of mine that were out there in the muck or up in the air as fighter pilots, you know. I wasn't out in the rice paddies trying to get shot at. Our base was getting mortared, but we were relatively safe.[35]

On the Vietnam War:

Our leadership through Vietnam was horrendous as far as the decisions that were made. Plus, the Vietnam vet has never been truly recognized for the tremendous courage he had in fighting an unpopular war.[36]

On family:

Living in a family is a real lesson in life. It teaches you things like love, respect, understanding, and the real meaning of sharing.[37]

On being a family man:

It is part of the responsibility of being a father and a husband to do things that your family likes to do. They enjoy being with you.[38]

On missing football:

I miss football more than I ever dreamed. It's like a part of your life that's gone forever, and you never stop missing it.[39]

NOTES

Chapter 1: The Cincinnati Kid
1. *Family Weekly*, November 22, 1964.
2. *Sport*, December 1964.

Chapter 2: Anchors Aweigh
1. *Sports Illustrated*, September 4, 1978.

Chapter 3: From Next Year's Champions to America's Team
1. *Fort Worth Star-Telegram*, August 2, 1985.
2. Skip Bayless, *God's Coach: The Hymns, Hype, and Hypocrisy of Tom Landry's Cowboys*. (New York: Simon and Schuster, 1990), p. 95.
3. *Dallas Morning News*, January 26, 1988, excerpted from *Dan Reeves with Dick Connor, Reeves: An Autobiography*.
4. Peter Golenbock, *Cowboys Have Always Been My Heroes*. (New York: Warner Books, 1997), p. 403.

5. Ibid., pp. 404-05.

6. Tom Landry, with Gregg Lewis, *Tom Landry: An Autobiography*. (Grand Rapids, MI: Zondervan; and New York: HarperCollins, 1990), p. 178.

7. Bob Hayes, with Robert Pack, *Run, Bullet, Run*. (New York: Harper and Row, 1990), p. 134.

8. Ibid., p. 135.

9. Landry and Lewis, *Tom Landry*, pp. 185-86.

10. Golenbock, *Cowboys Have Always Been My Heroes*, pp. 425-26.

11. Ibid., p. 365.

12. Ibid., p. 454.

13. Bayless, *God's Coach*, pp. 104-05.

14. Golenbock, *Cowboys Have Always Been My Heroes*, p. 486.

15. Ibid., p. 552.

16. Ibid., p. 551.

17. Landry and Lewis, *Tom Landry*, pp. 212-13.

18. Bayless, *God's Coach*, pp. 122-23.

19. Thomas "Hollywood" Henderson, and Peter Knobler, *Out of Control*. (New York: G. P. Putnam's Sons, 1987), p. 81.

20. Ibid., p. 101.

21. *Dallas Morning News*, December 24, 1995.

22. Ibid.

23. Ibid.

24. Ibid., January 26, 1988, excerpted from *Reeves: An Autobiography*.

25. Golenbock, *Cowboys Have Always Been My Heroes*, pp. 559-60.

26. Henderson and Knobler, *Out of Control*, pp. 126-27.

27. Golenbock, *Cowboys Have Always Been My Heroes*, pp. 611-12.

28. Henderson and Knobler, *Out of Control*, pp. 126-27.

29. Golenbock, *Cowboys Have Always Been My Heroes*, p. 667.

30. Bayless, *God's Coach*, p. 136.

Chapter 4: Roger da Man, In Demand

1. Bayless, *God's Coach: The Hymns, Hype, and Hypocrisy of Tom Landry's Cowboys.* New York: Simon and Schuster, 1990, p. 45.

2. *Dallas Morning News,* January 26, 1988, excerpted from *Reeves: An Autobiography.*

3. Thomas "Hollywood" Henderson, and Peter Knobler, *Out of Control,* New York: G. P. Putnam's Sons, 1987, p. 182.

4. *The New York Times,* July 22, 1984.

5. *Dallas Times Herald,* July 30, 1989.

6. Bloomberg.com, date unknown.

7. *Fort Worth Star-Telegram,* July 24, 1988.

8. Ibid., August 2, 1985.

9. *Sport,* December 1964.

Chapter 5: In His Own Words

1. *Houston Chronicle,* March 27, 1978.

2. Ibid.

3. Ibid.

4. *Athletes in Action,* Spring 1983.

5. Ibid.

6. *Saint Anthony Messenger,* September 1972.

7. Ibid.

8. Ibid.

9. Ibid.

10. *Columbia,* September 1977.

11. Ibid.

12. Skip Bayless, *God's Coach: The Hymns, Hype, and Hypocrisy of Tom Landry's Cowboys.* New York,: Simon and Schuster, 1990, p. 131; excerpted from his book *First Down, Lifetime to Go.*

13. *Saint Anthony Messenger,* September 1972.

14. *Sports Illustrated,* September 4, 1978.

15. Universal Press Syndicate, May 1980.

16. *Dallas Times Herald,* date unknown.

17. FamousTexans.com, date unknown.
18. *Dallas Morning News*, August 4, 1985.
19. *National Real Estate Investor*, October 1, 1999.
20. *Fort Worth Star-Telegram*, July 24, 1988.
21. Bayless, *God's Coach*, p. 120.
22. *Sports Illustrated*, September 4, 1978.
23. Ibid.
24. *The Sunday Capital*, December 19, 1993.
25. *Fort Worth Star-Telegram*, August 2, 1985.
26. *The Sunday Capital*, December 19, 1993.
27. *Sport*, December 1964.
28. Ibid.
29. Ibid.
30. Ibid.
31. *Sports Illustrated*, September 4, 1978.
32. Ibid.
33. Ibid.
34. Ibid.
35. *Fort Worth Star-Telegram*, August 2, 1985.
36. Ibid.
37. *Saint Anthony Messenger*, September 1972.
38. Ibid.
39. *Fort Worth Star-Telegram*, July 24, 1988.

GAME-BY-GAME
COLLEGE AND PRO FOOTBALL
CAREER STATS

1962
Navy (5-5)

Date	Opponent	Site	Result	Comp	Att	Pct	Yds	TDs	Int	Car	Yds	TDs
S22	Penn State	Away	L, 7-41	0	2	0.0	0	0	1	2	9	0
S29	Wm. & Mary	Home	W, 20-16	0	0	0.0	0	0	0	0	0	0
O6	Minnesota	Away	L, 0-21	0	2	0.0	0	0	0	2	-24	0
O13	Cornell	Home	W, 41-0	9	11	81.8	99	1	0	8	89	2
O20	Boston Col.	Away	W, 26-6	14	20	70.0	165	2	0	9	17	0
O27	Pittsburgh	Norfolk	W, 32-9	8	8	100.0	192	1	0	12	28	1
N3	Notre Dame	Phil.	L, 12-20	5	10	50.0	57	0	0	9	8	1
N10	Syracuse	Away	L, 6-34	9	15	60.0	159	1	2	10	-9	0
N17	Southern Cal	Away	L, 6-13	11	17	64.7	106	0	0	19	113	1
D1	Army	Phil.	W, 34-14	11	13	84.6	188	2	0	14	34	2
Totals				67	98	68.4	966	7	3	85	265	7

1963
Navy (9-2)

Date	Opponent	Site	Result	Comp	Att	Pct	Yds	TDs	Int	Car	Yds	TDs
S21	West Virginia	Away	W, 51-7	17	22	77.3	171	1	0	11	14	0
S28	Wm. & Mary	Home	W, 28-0	12	17	70.6	206	0	1	17	91	1
O5	Michigan	Away	W, 26-13	14	16	87.5	237	2	1	18	70	1
O11	SMU	Away	L, 28-32	12	22	54.5	128	1	1	18	107	1
O19	VMI	Norfolk	W, 21-12	9	13	69.2	148	0	0	19	-1	1
O26	Pittsburgh	Home	W, 24-12	14	19	73.7	168	0	0	19	-33	1
N2	Notre Dame	Away	W, 35-14	9	15	60.0	91	2	0	19	23	0
N9	Maryland	Home	W, 42-7	7	12	58.3	104	1	0	11	20	2
N16	Duke	Away	W, 38-25	7	14	50.0	122	0	1	12	72	1
D7	Army	Phil.	W, 21-15	6	11	54.5	99	0	2	12	55	0
Totals				107	161	66.4	1,474	7	6	156	418	8
J1	Texas (Cotton Bowl)		L, 6-28	21	31	67.7	228	0	1	12	-47	1

1964
Navy (3-6-1)

Date	Opponent	Site	Result	Comp	Att	Pct	Yds	TDs	Int	Car	Yds	TDs
S19	Penn State	Away	W, 21-8	5	13	38.5	44	0	0	12	-14	1
S26	Wm. & Mary	Home	W, 35-6	3	3	100.0	25	1	0	0	0	0
O3	Michigan	Away	L, 0-21	16	30	53.3	166	0	2	7	-3	0
O9	Georgia Tech	Jax'ville	L, 0-17	DNP								
O17	California	Away	L, 13-27	6	12	50.0	69	0	4	1	-23	0
O24	Pittsburgh	Away	T, 14-14	12	20	60.0	114	0	0	18	-37	0
O31	Notre Dame	Phil.	L, 0-40	19	36	52.8	155	0	1	19	12	0
N7	Maryland	Away	L, 22-27	25	39	64.1	231	3	2	13	-5	0
N14	Duke	Home	W, 27-14	21	30	70.0	217	0	1	17	91	1
N28	Army	Phil.	L, 8-11	12	21	57.1	110	0	0	17	-22	0
Totals				119	204	58.3	1,131	4	10	104	1	2
COLLEGIATE CAREER TOTALS				293	463	63.6	3,571	18	19	345	682	17

1969
Dallas Cowboys (11-2-1, Capitol Division first place)

Date	Opponent	Site	Start	Result	Comp	Att	Pct	Yds	TDs	Int
S21	St. Louis Cardinals	Home	Yes	W, 24-3	7	15	46.6	220	1	0
S28	New Orleans Saints	Away	DNP	W, 21-17						
O5	Philadelphia Eagles	Away	No	W, 38-7	5	8	62.8	60	0	1
O12	Atlanta Falcons	Away	No	W, 24-17	0	1	0.0	0	0	0
O19	Philadelphia Eagles	Home	No	W, 49-14	3	8	37.5	45	0	1
O27	New York Giants	Home	DNP	W, 25-3						
N2	Cleveland Browns	Away	No	L, 10-42	6	11	54.5	74	0	0
N9	New Orleans Saints	Home	DNP	W, 33-17						
N16	Washington Redskins	Away	DNP	W, 41-28						
N23	Los Angeles Rams	Away	DNP	L, 23-24						
N27	San Francisco 49ers	Home	DNP	T, 24-24						
D7	Pittsburgh Steelers	Away	DNP	W, 10-7						
D13	Baltimore Colts	Home	No	W, 27-10	2	4	50.0	22	0	0
D21	Washington Redskins	Home	DNP	W, 20-10						
Totals					23	47	48.9	421	1	2

Playoffs

Date	Opponent	Site	Start	Result	Comp	Att	Pct	Yds	TDs	Int
D28	Cleveland Browns	Home	No	L, 14-38	4	5	80.0	44	1	0
J3	Los Angeles Rams	Miami	No	L, 0-31	1	6	16.7	16	0	0

1970
Dallas Cowboys (10-4, NFC East first place)

Date	Opponent	Site	Start	Result	Comp	Att	Pct	Yds	TDs	Int
S20	Philadelphia Eagles	Away	Yes	W, 17-7	11	15	73.3	115	1	1
S27	New York Giants	Home	Yes	W, 28-10	13	23	56.5	133	1	1
O4	St. Louis Cardinals	Away	Yes	L, 7-20	2	6	33.3	16	0	2
O11	Atlanta Falcons	Home	DNP	W, 13-0						
O18	Minnesota Vikings	Away	No	L, 13-54	9	16	56.3	109	0	3
O25	Kansas City Chiefs	Away	DNP	W, 27-16						
N1	Philadelphia Eagles	Home	DNP	W, 21-17						
N8	New York Giants	Away	DNP	L, 20-23						
N16	St. Louis Cardinals	Home	No	L, 0-38	2	8	25.0	61	0	1
N22	Washington Redskins	Away	No	W, 45-21	2	5	40.0	26	0	0
N26	Green Bay Packers	Home	DNP	W, 16-3						
D6	Washington Redskins	Home	No	W, 34-0	3	4	75.0	66	0	0
D12	Cleveland Browns	Away	DNP	W, 6-2						
D20	Houston Oilers	Home	No	W, 52-10	2	5	40.0	16	0	0
Totals					44	82	53.7	542	2	8

Playoffs

Date	Opponent	Site	Start	Result
D26	Detroit Lions	Home	DNP	W, 5-0
J3	San Francisco 49ers	Away	DNP	W, 17-10

Super Bowl V

Date	Opponent	Site	Start	Result
J17	Baltimore Colts	Miami	DNP	L, 13-16

1971
Dallas Cowboys (11-3, NFC East first place)

Date	Opponent	Site	Start	Result	Comp.	Att.	Pct.	Yards	TDs	Int
S19	Buffalo Bills	Away	DNP	W, 49-37						
S26	Philadelphia Eagles	Away	Yes	W, 42-7	2	4	50.0	23	0	1
O3	Washington Redskins	Home	No	L, 16-20	6	9	66.7	103	0	0
O11	New York Giants	Home	Yes	W, 20-13	8	17	47.1	106	1	0
O17	New Orleans Saints	Away	No	L, 14-24	7	10	70.0	117	2	1
O24	New England Patriots	Home	Yes	W, 44-21	13	21	61.9	197	2	0
O31	Chicago Bears	Away	No	L, 19-23	7	11	63.6	87	0	1
N7	St. Louis Cardinals	Away	Yes	W, 16-13	20	31	64.5	199	1	0
N14	Philadelphia Eagles	Home	Yes	W, 20-7	14	28	50.0	176	0	0
N21	Washington Redskins	Away	Yes	W, 13-0	11	21	52.4	151	0	0
N25	Los Angeles Rams	Home	Yes	W, 28-21	8	14	57.1	176	2	0
D4	New York Jets	Home	Yes	W, 52-10	10	15	66.7	168	3	0
D12	New York Giants	Away	Yes	W, 42-14	10	14	71.4	232	3	0
D18	St. Louis Cardinals	Home	Yes	W, 31-12	10	16	62.5	147	1	1
Totals					126	211	59.7	1,882	15	4

Playoffs

Date	Opponent	Site	Start	Result	Comp.	Att.	Pct.	Yards	TDs	Int
D25	Minnesota Vikings	Away	Yes	W, 20-12	10	14	71.4	99	1	0
J2	San Francisco 49ers	Home	Yes	W, 14-3	9	15	60.0	163	0	0

Super Bowl VI

Date	Opponent	Site	Start	Result	Comp.	Att.	Pct.	Yards	TDs	Int
J16	Miami Dolphins	New Orleans	Yes	W, 24-3	12	19	63.2	119	2	0

1972
Dallas Cowboys (10-4, NFC East second place)

Date	Opponent	Site	Start	Result	Comp.	Att.	Pct.	Yards	TDs	Int
S17	Philadelphia Eagles	Home	DNP	W, 28-6						
S24	New York Giants	Away	DNP	W, 23-14						
O1	Green Bay Packers	Away	DNP	L, 13-16						
O8	Pittsburgh Steelers	Home	DNP	W, 17-13						
O15	Baltimore Colts	Away	DNP	W, 21-0						
O22	Washington Redskins	Away	DNP	L, 20-24						
O30	Detroit Lions	Home	DNP	W, 28-24						
N5	San Diego Chargers	Away	DNP	W, 34-28						
N12	St. Louis Cardinals	Home	DNP	W, 33-24						
N19	Philadelphia Eagles	Away	No	W, 28-7	1	3	33.3	16	0	1
N23	San Francisco 49ers	Home	No	L, 10-31	1	5	20.0	12	0	0
D3	St. Louis Cardinals	Away	No	W, 27-6	1	3	33.3	21	0	0
D9	Washington Redskins	Home	DNP	W, 34-24						
D17	New York Giants	Home	No	L, 3-23	6	9	66.7	49	0	1
Totals					**9**	**20**	**45.0**	**98**	**0**	**2**

Playoffs

D23	San Francisco 49ers	Away	No	W, 30-28	12	20	60.0	163	2	0
D31	Washington Redskins	Away	Yes	L, 3-26	9	20	45.0	98	0	0

1973
Dallas Cowboys (10-4, NFC East first place)

Date	Opponent	Site	Start	Result	Comp.	Att.	Pct.	Yards	TDs	Int
S16	Chicago Bears	Away	Yes	W, 20-17	9	22	40.9	91	2	2
S24	New Orleans Saints	Home	Yes	W, 40-3	10	15	66.7	124	1	1
S30	St. Louis Cardinals	Home	Yes	W, 45-10	17	22	77.3	276	2	0
O8	Washington Redskins	Away	Yes	L, 7-14	9	17	52.9	101	1	0
O14	Los Angeles Rams	Away	Yes	L, 31-37	15	25	60.0	173	2	3
O21	New York Giants	Home	Yes	W, 45-28	8	11	72.7	146	2	1
O28	Philadelphia Eagles	Away	Yes	L, 16-30	24	38	63.2	250	2	2
N4	Cincinnati Bengals	Home	Yes	W, 38-10	14	18	77.8	209	3	0
N11	New York Giants	Away	Yes	W, 23-10	7	16	43.8	76	1	0
N18	Philadelphia Eagles	Home	Yes	W, 31-10	7	16	43.8	108	2	3
N22	Miami Dolphins	Home	Yes	L, 7-14	15	24	62.5	155	0	1
D2	Denver Broncos	Away	Yes	W, 22-10	14	18	77.8	240	2	0
D9	Washington Redskins	Home	Yes	W, 27-7	16	25	64.0	223	0	2
D16	St. Louis Cardinals	Away	Yes	W, 30-3	14	19	73.7	256	3	0
Totals					**179**	**286**	**62.6**	**2,428**	**23**	**15**

Playoffs

D23	Los Angeles Rams	Home	Yes	W, 27-16	8	16	50.0	180	2	2
D30	Minnesota Vikings	Home	Yes	L, 10-27	10	21	47.6	89	0	4

1974
Dallas Cowboys (8-6, NFC East third place)

Date	Opponent	Site	Start	Result	Comp.	Att.	Pct.	Yards	TDs	Int
S15	Atlanta Falcons	Away	Yes	W, 24-0	13	27	48.1	252	1	0
S23	Philadelphia Eagles	Away	Yes	L, 10-13	19	33	57.6	217	0	2
S29	New York Giants	Home	Yes	L, 6-14	20	37	54.1	256	1	3
O6	Minnesota Vikings	Home	Yes	L, 21-23	9	20	45.0	144	2	4
O13	St. Louis Cardinals	Away	Yes	L, 28-31	19	29	65.5	236	1	1
O20	Philadelphia Eagles	Home	Yes	W, 31-24	18	27	66.7	224	0	0
O27	New York Giants	Away	Yes	W, 21-7	10	19	52.6	121	1	2
N3	St. Louis Cardinals	Home	Yes	W, 17-14	15	27	55.6	154	0	0
N10	San Francisco 49ers	Home	Yes	W, 20-14	9	14	64.3	177	0	0
N17	Washington Redskins	Away	Yes	L, 21-28	16	38	42.1	174	2	1
N24	Houston Oilers	Away	Yes	W, 10-0	8	15	53.3	69	0	0
N28	Washington Redskins	Home	Yes	W, 24-23	3	11	27.3	32	0	1
D7	Cleveland Browns	Home	Yes	W, 41-17	14	24	58.3	230	3	1
D14	Oakland Raiders	Away	Yes	L, 23-27	17	39	43.6	266	0	0
Totals					**190**	**360**	**52.8**	**2,552**	**11**	**15**

1975
Dallas Cowboys (10-4, NFC East second place)

Date	Opponent	Site	Start	Result	Comp.	Att.	Pct.	Yards	TDs	Int
S21	Los Angeles Rams	Home	Yes	W, 18-7	10	23	43.5	106	0	0
S28	St. Louis Cardinals	Home	Yes	W, 37-31	23	34	67.6	307	3	1
O6	Detroit Lions	Away	Yes	W, 36-10	11	18	61.1	212	2	2
O12	New York Giants	Away	Yes	W, 13-7	8	22	36.4	87	1	0
O19	Green Bay Packers	Home	Yes	L, 17-19	16	31	51.6	201	0	1
O26	Philadelphia Eagles	Away	Yes	W, 20-17	27	49	55.1	314	1	1
N2	Washington Redskins	Away	Yes	L, 24-30	17	29	58.6	217	2	1
N10	Kansas City Chiefs	Home	Yes	L, 31-34	17	31	54.8	243	2	2
N16	New England Patriots	Away	Yes	W, 34-31	10	14	71.4	190	3	0
N23	Philadelphia Eagles	Home	Yes	W, 27-17	11	15	73.3	155	0	2
N30	New York Giants	Home	Yes	W, 14-3	13	22	59.1	213	1	2
D7	St. Louis Cardinals	Away	Yes	L, 17-31	25	41	61.0	268	0	3
D13	Washington Redskins	Home	Yes	W, 31-10	10	19	52.6	153	2	1
D21	New York Jets	Away	DNP	W, 31-21						
Totals					**198**	**348**	**56.9**	**2,666**	**17**	**16**

Playoffs

D28	Minnesota Vikings	Away	Yes	W, 17-14	17	29	58.6	246	1	0
J4	Los Angeles Rams	Away	Yes	W, 37-7	16	26	61.5	220	4	1

Super Bowl X

J18	Pittsburgh Steelers	Miami	Yes	L, 17-21	15	24	62.5	204	2	3

1976
Dallas Cowboys (11-3, NFC East first place)

Date	Opponent	Site	Start	Result	Comp.	Att.	Pct.	Yards	TDs	Int
S12	Philadelphia Eagles	Home	Yes	W, 27-7	19	28	67.9	242	2	1
S19	New Orleans Saints	Away	Yes	W, 24-6	15	22	68.2	239	0	0
S26	Baltimore Colts	Home	Yes	W, 30-27	22	28	78.6	339	2	0
O3	Seattle Seahawks	Away	Yes	W, 28-13	14	20	70.0	200	2	1
O10	New York Giants	Away	Yes	W, 24-14	13	15	86.7	178	1	0
O17	St. Louis Cardinals	Away	Yes	L, 17-21	21	42	50.0	250	2	1
O24	Chicago Bears	Home	Yes	W, 31-21	12	21	57.1	162	1	0
O31	Washington Redskins	Away	Yes	W, 20-7	13	23	56.5	152	0	0
N7	New York Giants	Home	Yes	W, 9-3	13	25	52.0	161	0	1
N15	Buffalo Bills	Home	Yes	W, 17-10	15	34	44.1	202	1	0
N21	Atlanta Falcons	Away	Yes	L, 10-17	13	28	46.4	157	0	3
N25	St. Louis Cardinals	Home	Yes	W, 19-14	10	21	47.6	83	1	2
D5	Philadelphia Eagles	Away	Yes	W, 26-7	23	40	57.5	259	1	0
D12	Washington Redskins	Home	Yes	L, 14-27	5	22	22.7	91	1	2
Totals					208	369	56.4	2,715	14	11

Playoffs

Date	Opponent	Site	Start	Result	Comp.	Att.	Pct.	Yards	TDs	Int
D19	Los Angeles Rams	Home	Yes	L, 12-14	15	37	40.5	150	0	3

1977
Dallas Cowboys (12-2, NFC East first place)

Date	Opponent	Site	Start	Result	Comp.	Att.	Pct.	Yards	TDs	Int
S18	Minnesota Vikings	Away	Yes	W, 16-10	18	30	60.0	196	1	0
S25	New York Giants	Home	Yes	W, 41-21	18	29	62.1	235	1	0
O2	Tampa Bay Bucs	Home	Yes	W, 23-7	15	24	62.5	212	0	1
O9	St. Louis Cardinals	Away	Yes	W, 30-24	18	29	62.1	153	1	0
O16	Washington Redskins	Home	Yes	W, 34-16	15	28	53.6	250	2	0
O23	Philadelphia Eagles	Away	Yes	W, 16-10	15	26	57.7	172	0	0
O30	Detroit Lions	Home	Yes	W, 37-0	16	25	64.0	179	3	0
N6	New York Giants	Away	Yes	W, 24-10	14	25	56.0	190	1	0
N14	St. Louis Cardinals	Home	Yes	L, 17-24	11	20	55.0	102	1	2
N20	Pittsburgh Steelers	Away	Yes	L, 13-28	18	36	50.0	230	1	2
N27	Washington Redskins	Away	Yes	W, 14-7	10	24	41.7	138	1	1
D4	Philadelphia Eagles	Home	Yes	W, 24-14	13	26	50.0	183	1	2
D12	San Francisco 49ers	Away	Yes	W, 42-35	14	19	73.7	220	3	0
D18	Denver Broncos	Home	Yes	W, 14-6	15	20	75.0	160	2	1
Totals					210	361	58.3	2,620	18	9

Playoffs

Date	Opponent	Site	Start	Result	Comp.	Att.	Pct.	Yards	TDs	Int
D26	Chicago Bears	Home	Yes	W, 37-7	8	13	61.5	134	1	1
J1	Minnesota Vikings	Home	Yes	W, 23-6	12	23	52.2	165	1	1

Super Bowl XII

Date	Opponent	Site	Start	Result	Comp.	Att.	Pct.	Yards	TDs	Int
J15	Denver Broncos	New Orleans	Yes	W, 27-10	17	25	68.0	183	1	0

1978
Dallas Cowboys (12-4, NFC East first place)

Date	Opponent	Site	Start	Result	Comp.	Att.	Pct.	Yards	TDs	Int
S4	Baltimore Colts	Home	Yes	W, 38-0	16	22	72.7	280	4	2
S10	New York Giants	Away	Yes	W, 34-24	18	28	64.3	212	2	1
S17	Los Angeles Rams	Away	Yes	L, 14-27	22	46	47.8	246	2	4
S24	St. Louis Cardinals	Home	Yes	W, 21-12	16	26	61.5	182	1	0
O2	Washington Redskins	Away	Yes	L, 5-9	13	30	43.3	212	0	1
O8	New York Giants	Home	Yes	W, 24-3	17	32	53.1	246	3	1
O15	St. Louis Cardinals	Away	Yes	W, 24-21	23	40	57.5	289	3	2
O22	Philadelphia Eagles	Home	Yes	W, 14-7	10	22	45.4	108	1	0
O26	Minnesota Vikings	Home	Yes	L, 10-21	12	26	46.2	148	0	2
N5	Miami Dolphins	Away	Yes	L, 16-23	19	30	63.3	275	1	2
N12	Green Bay Packers	Away	Yes	W, 42-14	19	31	61.3	200	2	0
N19	New Orleans Saints	Home	Yes	W, 27-7	9	15	60.0	141	1	0
N23	Washington Redskins	Home	Yes	W, 37-10	9	19	47.4	218	1	1
D3	New England Patriots	Home	Yes	W, 17-10	15	27	55.6	243	2	0
D10	Philadelphia Eagles	Away	Yes	W, 31-13	13	19	68.4	190	2	0
D17	New York Jets	Away	DNP	W, 30-7						
Totals					231	413	55.9	3,190	25	16

Playoffs

Date	Opponent	Site	Start	Result	Comp.	Att.	Pct.	Yards	TDs	Int
D30	Atlanta Falcons	Home	Yes	W, 27-20	7	17	41.2	105	0	0
J7	Los Angeles Rams	Away	Yes	W, 28-0	13	25	52.0	176	2	2

Super Bowl XIII

Date	Opponent	Site	Start	Result	Comp.	Att.	Pct.	Yards	TDs	Int
J21	Pittsburgh Steelers	Miami	Yes	L, 31-35	17	30	56.7	228	3	1

1979
Dallas Cowboys (11-5, NFC East first place)

Date	Opponent	Site	Start	Result	Comp	Att	Pct	Yds	TDs	Int
S2	St. Louis Cardinals	Away	Yes	W, 22-21	20	34	58.8	269	0	0
S9	San Francisco 49ers	Away	Yes	W, 21-13	20	33	60.6	259	2	0
S16	Chicago Bears	Home	Yes	W, 24-20	18	31	58.1	222	3	0
S24	Cleveland Browns	Away	Yes	L, 7-26	21	39	53.9	303	1	2
S30	Cincinnati Bengals	Home	Yes	W, 38-13	12	25	48.0	164	2	1
O7	Minnesota Vikings	Away	Yes	W, 36-20	15	23	65.2	174	0	0
O14	Los Angeles Rams	Home	Yes	W, 30-6	13	18	72.2	176	3	0
O21	St. Louis Cardinals	Home	Yes	W, 22-13	11	25	44.0	164	2	2
O28	Pittsburgh Steelers	Away	Yes	L, 3-14	11	25	44.0	113	0	0
N4	New York Giants	Away	Yes	W, 16-14	20	30	66.7	266	1	0
N12	Philadelphia Eagles	Home	Yes	L, 21-31	17	28	60.7	308	3	0
N18	Washington Redskins	Away	Yes	L, 20-34	23	38	60.5	276	1	3
N22	Houston Oilers	Home	Yes	L, 24-30	21	30	70.0	287	2	2
D2	New York Giants	Home	Yes	W, 28-7	10	18	55.6	164	3	0
D8	Philadelphia Eagles	Away	Yes	W, 24-17	11	21	52.4	105	1	0
D16	Washington Redskins	Home	Yes	W, 35-34	24	42	57.1	336	3	1
Totals					267	461	57.9	3,586	27	11

Playoffs

Date	Opponent	Site	Start	Result	Comp	Att	Pct	Yds	TDs	Int
D30	Los Angeles Rams	Home	Yes	L, 19-21	13	28	46.4	124	1	1

CAREER REGULAR-SEASON TOTALS					1,685	2,958	57.0	22,700	153	109

INDEX

CPSIA information can be obtained
at www.ICGtesting.com
Printed in the USA
JSHW031036110221
11747JS00011B/10

9 781581 823059